CW01499869

THE MONSTER OF HARRODS

AL-FAYED, AND THE SECRET, SHAMEFUL HISTORY OF A BRITISH INSTITUTION

ALISON KERVIN

HarperCollins*Publishers*

Names marked with an asterisk and certain identifying details
have been changed to protect privacy.

HarperCollins*Publishers*
1 London Bridge Street
London SE1 9GF

www.harpercollins.co.uk

HarperCollins*Publishers*
Macken House, 39/40 Mayor Street Upper
Dublin 1, D01 C9W8, Ireland

First published by HarperCollins*Publishers* 2025

1 3 5 7 9 10 8 6 4 2

A catalogue record of this book is
available from the British Library

HB ISBN 978-0-00-875605-5
PB ISBN 978-0-00-876095-3

Printed and bound in the UK using 100%
renewable electricity at CPI Group (UK) Ltd

A NOTE FROM THE AUTHOR

This book contains language that readers may find offensive, including racist terminology and expressions. These terms have been included deliberately and with careful consideration, not to sensationalise or normalise such language but to accurately portray the historical realities and preserve the authenticity of the narrative. The inclusion of this offensive language is not intended to cause distress, but rather to confront the disturbing nature of the subject matter and to avoid sanitising history. The author neither endorses nor condones such language, nor the attitudes it represents.

For Peter & Cristine Kervin
& George Kervin-Evans

CONTENTS

THE FABRICATED PREFIX

He was born Mohamed Fayed, not Mohamed Al-Fayed. There was never an 'Al' in his name.

Like so many things about him, the 'Al' is entirely false and designed to impress. It's believed that he dreamt it up in the kitchen of the United Arab Emirates embassy in London in 1970 with Mahdi Al Tajir, the UAE's first ambassador to Britain, at the same time as they decided to take years off Fayed's age and create a more glamorous backstory for him.

The 'Al' was designed to hint that he came from a superior family, a bit like adding 'III' or 'IV' after your name to imply a long-established family lineage or announcing yourself as 'Williams of Highgrove' rather than 'Williams' to imply landed-gentry status when there is no historical connection to that estate. But Mohamed wasn't from Fayed, as the invented name implies, nor did he come from an elaborate Fayed dynasty. He was a crook, a charlatan, a bully and a rapist, so to afford him the dignity of an honour he does not deserve seems perverse.

His adopted name, resplendent with 'Al', is used in the subtitle of the book solely for the purpose of clarity. In what follows he will be plain old 'Fayed', unless his name is used in direct quotes by contributors to the book.

INTRODUCTION

THE HOUSE OF HORRORS

UNVEILING HARRODS'S DARK SECRET

'I have British kids, I provide employment for
thousands of people, my businesses pay millions and
millions in taxes, and I've given millions more to
charity. Anyone else would be thanked. Me?
I am brushed off as some upstart wog.'

Mohamed Fayed

Ah, poor, tormented Mohamed. The wounded victim, forever misunderstood.

When he died, in 2023, commentators rushed to praise him, lauding his flair for business and his unique charm. Michael Cole, his long-time spokesperson, described him as being 'full of great humanity', others rushed to comment on his kindness and generosity.

OK, so it might not have been quite the same as Tennyson carving 'a day when the whole world seemed to be darkness' into a rock when news of Lord Byron's death reached him, but praise for Fayed was pretty fulsome.

Then, everything changed. The dark truth was dragged kicking and screaming into the light thanks to reports from victims, galvanised by the BBC documentary *Al Fayed: Predator at Harrods*. Fayed wasn't a kind, compassionate man, he was one of the most vile predators and sexual abusers the world has known. He lied, deceived, cheated, abused, degraded, kidnapped and raped. The

BBC set the scene, and by the time you've finished reading this account, you'll realise that he was worse than you ever imagined. And yet he went to the grave believing that he'd been wronged, and that he deserved so much more love and attention.

My involvement began in early 2024, when three women separately confided in me about their traumatic experiences with Fayed. Their harrowing accounts were disturbingly similar – stories of humiliation, abuse and sexual assault at the hands of a man who wielded his power like a weapon. I listened, deeply moved by their courage and shaken by the weight of their trauma.

What troubled me was learning how others at the store had facilitated his behaviour over the decades, enabling these abuses while escaping any form of accountability themselves.

I began quietly researching, carefully documenting patterns and gathering information. Then came the BBC documentary. As the world watched in shock, I recognised the same patterns my friends had described – confirmation of what had been whispered about for years; these weren't isolated incidents but part of a systematic pattern of abuse spanning decades.

I spoke to another survivor, who in turn connected me with others. Each conversation revealed new horrors, but the methodical approach to abuse was the same – the grooming, the medical examinations, the NDAs, the threats. When 'Biggie', a former Harrods security guard, agreed to speak with me about what he had witnessed, I realised that this story demanded to be told in full – not just the what, but the how and why behind one of the most prolific predators of our time.

I've conducted sixty interviews with survivors, witnesses and former employees. I've pored over court documents, personnel files and hours of footage. I've spent extensive time with leading experts – including specialists in psychopathic behaviour and narcissistic personality disorder – seeking to understand not just what Fayed did, but the psychological mechanisms that drove him. What emerged from this research was not just a chronicle of abuse, but an examination of the systems and people that enabled it, offering insights into power dynamics and institutional failures that extend far beyond this single case.

Sitting across from women and men who still tremble when recounting their experiences, who still wake screaming from nightmares decades later, has been difficult. The extraordinary courage of these survivors, who, despite everything, were willing to relive their trauma in hope of finally being heard, should not be underestimated. Many have waited decades for acknowledgement, carrying their wounds in silence while their abuser was celebrated.

For twenty-five years Fayed was not only chairman but ringmaster of his golden playground in Knightsbridge. He'd stroll around the department store, accompanied by bagpipe players and a host of attractive women, smiling at pensioners, occasionally presenting them with £50 notes for no particular reason, and instructing his security officers to hand out lollipops to children (he didn't like to distribute them himself – children were full of germs, something that he absolutely couldn't abide). Mainly, though, on these ridiculous parades through his labyrinthine store, Fayed was looking for women to abuse.

Once he'd found a woman to his liking, whether a current member of staff or even a customer in the store, she'd be invited to come and work in his personal office. The characteristics needed for this were simple: she had to be English, blonde, tall, slim and pretty, preferably with a cut-glass accent. Once she was in place in the office, she would be persuaded to have an intimate medical. Then, when his doctors had deemed her clean and ready, he'd either rape or sexually abuse her.

This was the way he worked. Any messiness afterwards would be mopped up with NDAs, financial payoffs or sackings on trumped-up charges. Some members of the Metropolitan Police would assist him, if needed. The Harrods security teams had developed such close relationships with the forces of law and order that if fake 'arrests' needed to be made, these would pose absolutely no problem whatsoever. Fayed offered gifts and cash payments to the police in return for their cooperation, so nothing was out of reach.

Such was Fayed's ego that after he aggressively purchased Harrods, he set about turning the store into a tribute to himself and everything he stood for, a mausoleum to the gaudiness that he mistook for glamour

– the Egyptian escalator, the crypt in the basement, the visits from Michael Jackson . . . this 'glamour' knew no bounds.

But the greater the apparent grandeur, the greater the barbarity that was bubbling beneath the surface.

Today, even though Harrods was sold to the sovereign wealth fund of Qatar in 2010, and the Fayed family have no connection with the store, his reputation lingers over it with the reek of a carcass suspended from a butcher's hook. He has wrecked the reputation of the store he so desired that he cheated and lied to get it. Fayed didn't so much put a match to the good name of Harrods; he set light to its reputation with a flamethrower. Who now would want to stride through Knightsbridge clutching a Harrods carrier bag? It's about as appealing as wearing a *Jim'll Fix It* badge or a Gary Glitter T-shirt.

Those running Harrods today have been clear that they are 'utterly appalled by the allegations of abuse' and they insist that Harrods is very different from the Harrods that operated under Fayed.

But there's no question that by the time he walked out of the doors for the last time, Fayed had wrung every last ounce of joy out of the place and caused hundreds of people irreparable damage due to his selfish desire for power and control. He would strut around the store, sacking anyone who failed to meet his exacting standards of beauty and comportment while he was the embodiment of every characteristic he loathed in others – too dark, too small, too bald, too ugly. He had the whole damn lot.

Fayed stands alone in his guilt for the crimes he committed, but he did not commit them alone, and we will therefore look at the people who enabled him to behave so appallingly: the doctors, the security officers, the management, the secretaries, drivers and doormen, all those who stood by and said nothing while people suffered. Why did they do this? Why did people say nothing? What psychological explanations – bystander effect, perhaps, or the theory of creeping ethics – can shed light on what happened?

Fayed was a power-hungry abuser, a tyrant in a tailored suit, a Henry VIII for the modern era. But where the Tudor king beheaded women, Fayed destroyed them. Where Henry dissolved monasteries, Fayed demolished anyone who questioned his authority. Both men commanded absolute deference, rewrote inconvenient truths and built empires on the backs of the terrified. These were two outsiders who seized power and wielded it without mercy, determined to force history itself to validate their existence.

Fayed loved to shove money down women's blouses and throw expensive gifts around, but his gift-giving was a means of control and a demonstration of power, not largesse. He never gave to give; he gave to receive. He understood that power wasn't merely about wealth or titles but about controlling the narrative – he built monuments, spun conspiracies and leveraged his wealth to craft the story of a man wronged by an empire.

When tragedy struck in the Pont de l'Alma tunnel in 1997, claiming the lives of his son Dodi and Princess

Diana, Fayed didn't merely grieve – he seized the moment to cement himself within British history. The shrine he erected in Harrods wasn't just a memorial; it was a declaration of war against the Establishment, part of his battle against the royal family, even though his son had only been dating Diana for a matter of weeks before they died.

The way in which he pointed the finger at Prince Philip in the most hideous way, accusing him of murdering his own daughter-in-law with absolutely no evidence, was indefensible. The horrible truth is that they were killed by a drunk driver employed by Fayed, taking the couple from a hotel owned by Fayed on their way to his son's apartment, also owned by Fayed. The royal family were nowhere near the whole thing.

But that didn't stop Fayed from sitting in the privacy of his opulent office and criticising the royal family, accusing them of murder. When people stopped listening to his moaning, he tore the royal warrants off Harrods's frontage to attract more headlines.

This is not a biography of Fayed. Instead it aims to lift the curtain and look at what went on during all those years at the department store he owned, asking why on earth Fayed behaved like he did and how he was allowed to do so. It also looks at his family; his two brothers, Ali and Salah, now stand accused of rape too. All three men are accused in these pages of a string of heinous crimes over many years, including passing women between them, drugging them and raping them.

One woman I spoke to was forced to have an abortion, and there are dozens of stories from women who were so badly hurt that they considered taking their own lives. One was warned by Omar, Fayed's son, that she should keep away from his 'dangerous' father, another was saved by an older lady called Barbara who fought to keep the young and pretty girls out of Fayed's clutches. There are very few good people in this tale, but these two lift the story out of the cesspit.

What makes the story of Mohamed Fayed and Harrods burst with emotion is the raw humanity of these testimonies, the trembling voices and haunted eyes of people still carrying wounds decades old.

There is racism on an unprecedented scale, there are secretaries being made to crawl on the floor like donkeys and bray loudly while their employer laughed, as well as workers being framed and then threatened by the very person they were working for. And although Fayed physically attacked women, men weren't spared his evil touch. In what follows we will examine the way he humiliated virtually all his staff, sacking those who failed to reach the standards he demanded of everyone save himself.

He told one man to walk around the office naked from the waist down. The man did as he was told and was sacked for gross misconduct. If the man had not done his boss's bidding, he would have been sacked for insubordination. This is one of many Catch-22 situations into which Fayed threw the people he employed. No one could win.

The man was a mess of inconsistencies. When he first arrived in London in the 1960s, he seemed on the surface to be a jolly clown – an unpredictable, fun-loving foreigner who'd come to Britain to spend his wealth, make friends and brighten newspaper headlines. With his boisterous outbursts and shaking jowls he was like an Egyptian Colonel Blimp, overweight and pompous, strutting around his department store, throwing out demands, forever changing his mind and blaming everyone else for everything that went wrong. Sure, he was crass and crude, producing vibrators in business meetings, handing over pretend Viagra like a teenager and discussing his sex life with anyone who'd listen, but most people laughed along. When he slipped a boxful of lobsters into the boot of Virginia Bottomley's ministerial car while she was in Harrods, everyone laughed. Even his appearance on the TV show *Being Bobby Brown* in which he gave Viagra to Whitney Houston was met with smiles and laughter.

But there was a much darker side – after death the mask fell off and he was revealed to be an evil, cowardly abuser of women and manipulator of people. That mask was slipping while he was still alive, people had a glimpse of what the man was really like, but most did nothing. You'll read in these pages of the devastating consequences of their silence. Police are investigating those at Harrods who assisted Fayed and helped him to cause such extraordinary damage to so many people.

It's a travesty that Fayed himself isn't alive to hear the universal roar of anger and suffer the consequences of his actions. It's a bitter injustice that he's not locked in a cell, watching on as his reputation and everything he worked for burns in front of him.

What compelled me to bring this story to light wasn't just journalistic curiosity, but a deep sense of responsibility to those who had been silenced for too long. In the survivors who trusted me with their stories, I saw not just victims of one man's depravity, but the devastating failure of multiple institutions meant to protect them.

This book offers more than just an account of Fayed's crimes. Through the insights of psychologists and experts I consulted, it provides a window into how power corrupts, how institutions fail their most vulnerable members, and how predators identify, isolate and manipulate their victims. The patterns revealed here transcend this specific case, offering vital lessons about the structures that enable abuse across society.

But at its heart, this is a book about courage – the courage of survivors who have stepped forward to reclaim their narratives from a man who tried to reduce them to objects. Their testimony stands as both an indictment of the past and a warning for the future. Their bravery demands nothing less than our complete attention.

1

SCENTED PREY

THE GIRLS ON THE PERFUME COUNTER

'No woman wants to have her rapist's baby.'

Belinda

LIZ

It's the trickle of blood that she remembers. Liz lay still as it traced a slow path across the contours of her cheek before pooling at the edge of her jawline. Afraid to move lest it provoke him, she lay barely breathing, willing it to be over.

Mohamed Fayed, owner of Harrods and the most terrifying man she'd ever encountered, sat next to her. She glanced at his crumpled face and saw a look of disgust spread across it as the blood began to drip onto his expensive white sheets.

'I was worried that he'd get violent,' she recalls. 'He looked so angry about the blood that I felt guilty. The man had just raped me but I was shaking with fear about the consequences for the bed sheets. That's what he did to you. That was the impact he had.'

Fayed eased himself to his feet, pulled his bathrobe around him, looked down at her and told her to leave. 'He watched me while I struggled into my clothes. He kept staring at me all the time.'

The staring was nothing new. Liz recalls him watching her from the day she started working at the Knightsbridge store in 1994. He observed her when she walked around the sales floor, when she stepped out of the lift and when she talked to customers.

'He was like a wild animal stalking its prey.'

Liz had been working at Harrods for three weeks when the rape took place in Fayed's apartment. Looking back, she can see that the process of grooming her started from the moment she caught his eye when she was shopping in the store with her friend Claire.

'He was on one of his grand tours of the store, with his entourage. We stopped to watch him go past and were flattered when he came and talked to us. He asked us what we did, and we said we'd just finished our A Levels. He asked whether we wanted to work at Harrods. Just like that. He didn't know anything about us, but thought we'd fit in. He told us that the money was very good and he'd look after us. I said that sounded great. A woman who was walking round with him took my details, then he squeezed my cheek and told me to come in on Monday.

'I turned to Claire and said, "He just touched my cheek." Honestly, I could feel myself going bright red. I remember the excitement, even now – I remember the thrill of it all. I'd never met a celebrity. I was a kid. Things like that don't happen to you when you're a schoolgirl from Essex. I was dying to tell everyone about it.'

Claire wasn't interested in joining her, so it was Liz – all on her own – who arrived at 9 o'clock the following Monday morning, eager to work in the world's most famous store.

Little did she realise, on that sunny day in July, that her world was about to tilt on its axis. The meeting with Fayed had started a chain of events that would result in such a dent to her confidence and trust in people that her life would never be the same again.

'I'd been told what to wear – a white blouse and black skirt. But I was reprimanded because my shoes were too high and I wasn't wearing enough make-up. "The chairman doesn't like high-heeled shoes," they said. I heard that a lot. I don't know whether it was because he was short. I guess so. Or he might have had a thing about them. I don't know, but I promised I'd get some flat shoes and I was told I'd be working on the perfume counter.'

Liz recalls walking out onto the ground floor and joining the others assembled there. She says they were all young, attractive and very glamorous. She was told to go through to the cosmetics area and make herself up.

'I didn't think I'd ever see the boss again, but he appeared after a few hours and asked me how I was settling in. I was surprised by how much attention he paid me. I was the lowest of the low in terms of pecking order, but he always came to find me and say hello.'

Liz had no idea of the frightening truth behind the friendly waves and affectionate smiles. When she was asked to go up to his apartment a few weeks later, she thought it 'odd, but not madly so. I thought he was going to ask me how I was getting on.'

She was met by one of his assistants, who took her to Fayed. The assistant knocked on the door and Liz was summoned inside. Fayed told her that she was very beautiful and looked much better with make-up. He said he wanted her to talk about what it had been like working at Harrods, and whether she was happy in the perfume department. He was thinking of moving her to his personal office. What did she think about that?

'I'd only been there for three weeks, and had no complaints, so I told him I was happy. Then he asked whether I would mind if he made a video of me saying how much I enjoyed working at Harrods.' She said that was fine, but noted how odd it felt that Fayed himself was setting up the tripod and organising the filming. He couldn't walk around the store unaccompanied, he had hundreds of assistants and a huge PR and marketing team, but he was making this video himself. He told her that the light was much better in the bedroom and suggested she sit on the bed while he filmed her.

'I'd hardly entered the bedroom when he lunged at me. I thought he'd fallen when he rushed in and pushed me back, but then he shoved his hand up my skirt and it became obvious what was happening. I froze to start with – I felt I had no strength at all – then I tried to fight back. I shouted out, and he put his hand over my mouth. I was kicking and pushing, but I couldn't stop him. He raped me.'

Bloodied and crying, and still clambering back into her clothes, she ran out of Fayed's sumptuous top-floor apartment and down the corridor, before heading back into the store. She ran into the ladies' toilets, let herself into a cubicle and collapsed, crying. She had no idea what to do. She cleaned herself up and returned to the perfume floor, where she tried to shut out what had just happened. She avoided eye contact and carried on with her work.

At 3 o'clock that afternoon she was organising stock and talking to customers when she saw two security officers walking towards her, side by side, in perfect unison, like soldiers marching to an imaginary drumbeat. One of them asked her to come with them. She said she couldn't because she was the only one on the counter. They took an arm each, marched her through the store in front of everyone and led her down to the basement, where she was put in a small, windowless room they all referred to as 'the cell'.

'I was terrified. I didn't know what I'd done wrong, but was too scared to ask. My overwhelming fear was that I was going to be raped again. My legs shook and I could hear my heart beating in my ears. Then another security officer came in. He handed me my coat and said they had reason to believe that I'd stolen from the store. They looked through the coat in front of me and showed me a bottle of perfume that I'd allegedly stolen.

'I screamed at them that I hadn't stolen it and burst into tears. I couldn't believe what was happening. I was taken over to a table and told that I could either be given a sum of money, sign a non-disclosure agreement and leave, or they'd ring the police, who would arrest me.' Liz chose the former, and departed that day with £250 cash, a non-disclosure agreement and all her trust gone forever.

The attack left Liz bruised and bleeding, but it's the psychological damage that has left handprints much uglier and more enduring than the physical marks on her body. When she goes to sleep at night, she feels his hands around her throat and feels bile and terror rising inside her. The memory of her blood – slowly trickling onto expensive white sheets while her throat is being squeezed – keeps her awake long into the early hours, many years after the incident, and it flashes into her mind when she least expects it.

The 'fake theft' arrangement that Liz endured as a means to get her out of the building while keeping her quiet was certainly not something new for Fayed, who moved quickly to remove from his services anyone who was likely to cross him or reveal what he'd done. NDAs given to terrified young women kept them quiet, but Fayed had other tools at his disposal. Had Liz opted for the police option, she would have been arrested on trumped-up charges, such was the power and control that Fayed exerted over the Metropolitan Police, something which happened to many women over the course of Fayed's reign.

BELINDA

Belinda's experiences at Harrods also scarred her for life. 'I wouldn't be exaggerating if I said that Fayed ruined everything for me, forever, the day he raped me,' she said.

Like dozens of other women, she was working on the perfume floor when she found herself at the centre of Fayed's fantasies. Indeed, the floor was known as 'the sweet shop' because Fayed would go there to pick out which sweets he wanted that day. It was where the 'pretty people' worked. There was even a recruitment agency that offered part-time work to models and actresses between jobs. All the recruits from there went to work on the perfume counter with women like Liz and Belinda.

'It all started when the chairman's personal assistant called me and asked me to come into his office,' said Belinda. 'I got there, and he said he wanted to find out whether I was happy.'

Like Liz, she was astonished that he would bother with someone so junior. 'He seemed genuinely impressed with me, and said he could get me a job in the buying department, which was something I desperately wanted. I thought he was wonderful. I took it all as a compliment and as a sign that I was doing well.'

A few days later, she was told her that she was being moved to the buying department. 'I couldn't believe what I was hearing. It was something I'd always wanted. I was taken up to the offices, given a desk and a computer, and told that I was now a buyer. I sat there unsure what to do.'

A few days later she was invited to go to Fayed's private apartment. She thought he might explain what the new role involved. 'When I look back now, I wish I'd spoken to someone . . . anyone. But I didn't. I just went up to his apartment and I was raped by him.'

It's nearly thirty years since that day, but Belinda is still deeply affected by it. She cries throughout the interview, rising to walk around the room, shaking her head as if trying to release the memory of it all. She says that after the rape, she fled the apartment 'past security guards', and ran home.

The following morning she called in sick, and when she went in the morning after that, her desk had disappeared and she'd been moved from her glitzy role in the buying department back to working on the sales floor. 'I was soiled goods,' she says. 'I was made to feel disgusting, and I'd done nothing wrong other than be attacked by this man. You'd think I had attacked him rather than the other way round.'

Two months went by, with Belinda hiding whenever Fayed went past on his store walks. 'I was worried that if he saw me there, he might sack me, so I hid whenever he went past.'

One day Belinda realised it had been ages since she'd had a period. They were always reliable and on time, but she hadn't had one since the rape by Fayed. 'I knew. I just knew. I went to the chemists and bought a pregnancy testing kit. I remember tearing the box to get it open. Minutes later I watched as a clear blue line appeared. It was positive. I hadn't slept with anyone for months. I knew it must be my rapist's child. I felt scared, alone and terrified. I kept thinking that maybe the test was wrong. Should I have bought another one? Perhaps I should have bought another one?

'It was then that I made the most stupid mistake of my life. I went to see Dr Wendy Snell, the Harrods doctor. I told her I might be pregnant and she gave me a test to do. When it came back positive, I burst into tears and explained what had happened. 'She told me that I should keep quiet about it and she'd arrange for me to have an abortion. Harrods would pay for it, and no one would ever find out. She told me to come back the next day and it would be arranged. All I had to do was sign an NDA and the rest would be taken care of. At no time did she say, "Do you want this baby?" That wasn't on the cards because it wouldn't have suited the chairman, and his views were all that mattered.

'I didn't go back the next day . . . I felt too nervous and confused. Instead I phoned in sick and made a plan to meet a friend in a café to tell her what had happened and see what she thought I should do. I left home around 11 a.m. to go and meet her, and realised straight away that I was being followed. As I got to the café in Putney, two men approached me. I recognised one of them from the store. I now know that his name was John Macnamara [head of Harrods security].'

The security officers told her that she'd be given money for an abortion and needed to sign an NDA. She said she wanted to talk to someone first.

'They turned nasty then, and said there was no time to mess around and I had to sign it straight away. One of them – I think it was John Macnamara – said he knew where my parents lived and would cause trouble for me if I breathed a word about this to anyone. I was basically made to sign the NDA, then they said I was to leave for work as usual the next morning, and they would meet me at the corner of my road and accompany me to have an abortion.

'I was too terrified to tell anyone about what happened, and I haven't told anyone to this day. My parents are both alive and neither of them knows. I went with the guys the next morning and I had the abortion, and they gave me an envelope with £1,000 in it and told me I no longer had a job. I went home and I've never been back to Harrods since.

'Losing a baby like that was hard. No woman wants to have her rapist's baby, but I never had children. Things never worked out in that way. I was scarred by what I went through, and I sometimes think about how different my life might have been if I'd never gone to work at Harrods.'

It wasn't until Belinda saw the 2024 BBC documentary *Al Fayed: Predator at Harrods*, which exposed the level of abuse that had taken place, that she realised she'd not been alone. 'I watched the documentary and I couldn't process what I was seeing. I think I had a minor break-down afterwards. The fact that the doctor was in on it and was acting against my best interests was just awful. All of those people conspiring against me, all of them making sure he was never caught. That vile organisation headed by a monster. It makes me want to scream and lash out. I wish he was still alive. I wish we could all go and kill him.'

Belinda's hands are balled up. 'How did he get away with it? How does one man get away with decades of abusing women and never get caught? How?'

2

SAND TO SKYSCRAPERS

THE EGYPTIAN ORIGINS

'I warned you you'd regret it. Have you
noticed that I'm always there?'

Fayed to Sheenagh, after she rejected him

When Fayed arrived in London in 1965, he was a thirty-six-year-old conman with a fabricated backstory and a willingness to tell whatever lies he needed to in order to ingratiate himself with British society. He had a false name, a false date of birth and such a complicated relationship with the truth there was every chance he'd long since lost the ability to separate fact from fiction.

He presented himself as a man of great wealth, breeding and sophistication, but the bare facts are that he was born in the Gomrok slum in Alexandria in Egypt, within sight of the exclusive Yacht Club where the elite gathered, but far enough away to know his place in society. The view of that club from the squalor of Gomrok, represented everything he desired. It would become a powerful metaphor for his life.

He was born on 2 January 1929 (although he claimed that he was born later) to Hanem Kotb Hassan and Aly Aly Fayed, a schoolteacher who went on to become a school inspector. The third of five children, his two sisters were born first, then Mohamed, followed by Salah, two years later, and Ali two years after that.

Soon after Ali's birth, his mother died, leaving five young children motherless and grief-stricken. Aly Aly found himself thrown into the role of mother and father; he needed to carry on earning a living while giving time and energy to looking after his children; they needed to be consoled, loved and protected. It was a role he was entirely unsuited to, and his lack of empathy in these crucial early years would put a wedge between father and son that lasted a lifetime.

Aly Aly coped with his new life by imposing the strictest of rules on his young children to keep them in order and the household running smoothly. There was no time for warmth and tenderness, no time for play or even home-work, as the children did all the chores and kept the household running as their mother had done. If anything was amiss, not cleaned properly or not tended to, they would suffer the wrath of their father.

The psychological impact of the lack of affection from his father cannot be overstated. The young boy had formed deep bonds of attachment to his mother but lacked the emotional tools to process his grief, creating an 'emotional hole'. An adult can spend a lifetime trying to fill this void with external achievements, possessions and status, and create a relentless drive for wealth and recognition. An 'emotional hole' can also create a complicated relationship with truth, where fantasy becomes a protective mechanism against painful reality.

In 1939, when Mohamed was ten years old and war was breaking out in Europe, his father found a new partner and remarried. The whole family – father, stepmother and five children – moved to a bigger flat in the same run-down area of Alexandria.

One may imagine that having a female influence back in the family home would have restored balance, but it did nothing to help young Fayed who disliked his new home, missed his mother and despised his stepmother. But his greatest vitriol was reserved for his father, whom he saw as controlling in the home but weak and unambitious in public.

Fayed's resentment towards his father and stepmother is understandable. A grief counsellor suggested that 'the new mother figure in his life may well be seen as an intruder, and he may resent his dad for moving on so quickly. These circumstances would produce a boy who was prematurely emotionally self-sufficient. This, in turn, would lead to the development of compensatory mechanisms such as grandiosity, controlling behaviours and an insatiable need for external validation – traits that would become hallmarks of Fayed's adult personality.'

Growing up during the British occupation, Fayed observed the stark power imbalances that defined his world. Alexandria in the 1930s and 40s was a city divided, not just between rich and poor, but between coloniser and colonised. The city had a cosmopolitan character, with substantial European communities full of people who often held privileged positions, while many native

Egyptians, particularly those from poorer backgrounds, experienced discrimination and limited opportunities. This social hierarchy was reinforced by colonial policies that favoured British and European interests.

For someone like Fayed, growing up in this environment, the power dynamics of colonial rule would have been visible in everyday life through segregated spaces, economic disparities, and social hierarchies that placed Europeans (particularly the British) at the top of the social order.

A substantial military garrison was stationed in Alexandria and immaculately uniformed British officers dominated the area, provoking a combination of reluctant respect and simmering resentment. British officers strolled through the streets with unwavering confidence while Egyptian children, Fayed among them, hastily cleared their path. The officers frequented exclusive establishments where Egyptians could enter only in service capacities, reinforcing the differences. For a boy of boundless ambition but limited prospects, the contrast between his circumstances and those of the British elite created a complex emotional blueprint. Egypt during this period was a society simultaneously resentful of and fascinated by British colonial power. Young Fayed admired the wealth and status of the British, while harbouring resentment at their dominance over his homeland.

Contrary to the successful business background he would later fabricate, Fayed's commercial journey began modestly, peddling Coca-Cola bottles on street corners when he was nineteen, progressing to knocking on doors, selling Singer sewing machines by the time he was twenty-one. 'I started with nothing, selling Coca-Cola on the streets of Alexandria,' Fayed once acknowledged in a rare moment of candour during a 1985 interview with *The Sunday Times*. 'You learn business from the ground up that way, you understand what makes people buy.'

Fayed seemed destined for a life as a street seller scraping together enough money to feed himself, but it was a friendship that saved him. His friend Tousson El Barrawi lived in an apartment next to a seventeen-year-old called Adnan Khashoggi and the two had decided to start a business, for which they sought an employee.

Khashoggi is best-known in the West as an extravagant, billionaire arms dealer who acted as an intermediary between Western defence companies and the Saudi government.

As a teenager, Adnan was encouraged by his father Mohamed Khashoggi, the King of Saudi Arabia's personal physician, to start a business furnishing the homes and surgeries of doctors moving to Saudi Arabia from Egypt. The business was conceived at a time when oil money in Saudi was increasing, and professionals were heading to the country in greater numbers than ever, to earn bigger salaries than they could at home. All the equipment and furniture would be shipped from Egypt.

This business was to be run by Tousson, Adnan and his cousin, Anas Yassin. But they needed someone based in Jeddah in Saudi Arabia to oversee things and take delivery of the furniture they shipped over. This was the role they offered to Fayed in 1952. The new job would involve relocating to Saudi Arabia, of course, but the money was good. Fayed would be paid E£100 per month and 9 per cent of the company's profits. This was over ten times what he had been making as a sewing machine salesman.

The other advantage of this job was that he would be employed directly by Mohamed Khashoggi in order to overcome any problems with a work visa, so he would be thrown into Khashoggi senior's glamorous world, where he would learn a huge amount and have the opportunity to impress with his hard work.

SAUDI ARABIA

Fayed became hugely popular during his time in Saudi Arabia and was credited with making the company a success. Khashoggi gave him other projects to work on, and Fayed responded by making a success of them, too. One of those projects was Belrock, a company that extracted gypsum in the desert. By the end of his first year in the job, Fayed had made around $300,000 profit.

He travelled back to Alexandria periodically to liaise with Adnan and Yassin over the long-term future of the company, and on one trip he met Samira Khashoggi, Adnan's younger sister. They began dating, she moved to Saudi Arabia, and in July 1954 they were married. The next year, their son Emad was born, known throughout his life as Dodi.

But the marriage didn't last long. Fayed's unfaithfulness, coupled with Samira's realisation that she was in love with her cousin, Anas Yassin, brought the marriage to a swift conclusion.

The break-up of the relationship also signalled the end of his ties with the Khashoggis for the next few years, meaning his access to wealth and contacts was shut down. He came to an agreement with the family that he would be paid 50,000 Saudi riyals and 2 per cent of any future profits in Belrock, the company he'd worked for. But the situation was complicated when the Khashoggis realised Fayed had secretly withdrawn E£100,000 from the company's bank account. It was an extraordinary betrayal, considering everything their family had done for him. They contacted him, asking him to return the stolen money and he refused. So, in 1958, Fayed received his first writ.

The situation was resolved when Fayed struck a deal: he'd allow Samira to remarry and return to Egypt in return for the money he owed. Prior to that, she'd been forced to remain in Saudi Arabia and was unable to marry. Samira went on to marry her cousin.

Now Fayed had finished working for the Khashoggis, he returned to Alexandria, bought a huge house and began to establish himself as a businessman in his own right.

He had won custody of Dodi in the divorce from Samira, as is customary in Egyptian law, but there was no room in his plans for a needy child, so he left his son with his brother Salah, who in turn left Dodi to be brought up by various members of staff.

Dodi saw very little of his mother or father in his form-ative years. He once claimed, to his ex-wife Susanne Gregard, to whom he was married for eight months in the 1980s, that he didn't meet his mother until he was fifteen, but there are photographs of him with his mother when he was five or six years old, so it's likely that he just felt as if he hadn't seen his mother for his entire childhood.

He once told Gregard that he was a Catholic, not a Muslim. She mused that 'maybe the help in the house was Catholic', hinting at both the lack of religion in the house, and the amount of time Dodi was left with staff rather than his parents.

Certainly, his father spent very little time with Dodi, and this abandonment created a complex and fraught relationship between father and son that would endure until Dodi's death. Although Fayed would later portray himself as a devoted father, the reality was far more complicated. Dodi grew up with a phantom father who materialised occasionally with extravagant gifts but was absent for the daily intimacies of parenting. Fayed's reck-less, unloving approach to Dodi is eerily reminiscent of Fayed's own treatment at the hands of his father when he was a child.

It's important to note that Egypt was a society that was deeply inequitable. The role of fathers in parenting was reduced to wage-earning and exacting discipline on chil-dren. 'Women were there to look after children. That's all women were seen to be good for – looking after the home, bringing up the children and keeping out of the way of the men who were deemed to be far superior beings,' says Doha Gamal, an academic at the University of Cairo.

Even today, according to the Global Gender Gap Index, Egypt ranks 134th and 140th out of 153 countries in women's economic participation and opportunity respectively. Only 18 per cent of working-age women participated in the economy, compared with 65 per cent of men. It's also worth mentioning that sexual harassment is endemic. The Egyptian Centre for Women's Rights have found that 98 per cent of foreign women and 83 per cent of native women said they had been sexually harassed in Egypt, with two-thirds of men admitting they had harassed women. This cultural context may provide some insight into the attitudes towards women that would later characterise Fayed's behaviour at Harrods. Growing up in a society where women were marginalised and objectified inevitably shaped his views.

After being expelled from the influential Khashoggi family circle in 1956, Fayed needed to establish himself independently. His patterns of behaviour over the next decade would follow a common course: ingratiate himself with powerful figures, profit from these connections, engage in questionable practices and leave when circumstances turned against him.

HAITI

After fleeing from his homeland, Fayed's next adventure came in Haiti. This period represents his first major attempt at wholesale self-transformation, an experiment in creating a new identity in a place where no one knew his origins. He introduced himself to everyone as 'Sheikh Mohamed Fayed' and told Papa Doc Duvalier, the brutal dictator, that he could bring Middle Eastern riches to the impoverished island if he was allowed to build an oil refinery and develop the wharf at Port-au-Prince.

Papa Doc believed him; a contract with an American firm was cancelled, and Fayed was given the job. Before long he found himself being driven around in a limousine protected by the feared Tonton Macoute bodyguards and clutching a diplomatic passport. Much of the information about Fayed's time in Haiti comes from Raymond Joseph, an incredible man who ran for president of Haiti, translated the Bible into Creole, wrote for the *Wall Street Journal* and launched the country's first weekly newspaper – the *Haïti Observateur*.

Joseph worked hard to make life easier and better for Haitians struggling under Papa Doc's tyrannical reign. He attacked Papa Doc in print, making a lifelong enemy of him, and was on the 'hit list' of both Papa Doc and his son, Jean-Claude Duvalier, commonly known as 'Baby Doc'. It's difficult to resist comparing Joseph, whose mission was to make life better for those less fortunate, with Fayed, whose life goal appears to have been precisely the opposite: to ignore any pain and suffering on his road to earning as much money, power and influence as possible, while issuing a constant stream of lies to ease his passage.

Joseph says that Fayed became engaged to one of Papa Doc's daughters, and that was how he became so close to the leader and so influential in the country. But he wasn't influential for long. Fayed had convinced Papa Doc Duvalier that he could discover oil in Haiti and develop it for the country's benefit, part of his grand promise about bringing Middle Eastern wealth to the impoverished island.

During one of his 'explorations', Fayed triumphantly announced he'd discovered oil. What he had actually found was molasses from an old sugar refinery. This humiliating mistake, combined with financial deception (Fayed claimed he'd invested $4 million in Haiti and that the government owed him money, but the truth was that he stole around $150,000 from them), severely damaged his relationship with the Duvalier regime. The situation became increasingly dangerous for him as Papa Doc and his notorious death squads, the Tonton Macoutes, realised they'd been deceived. Fayed did what he did best – he ran away, this time heading for Europe, then on to the UK.

LONDON

London in the mid-1960s was transitioning from grim post-war austerity to the glamour and glitz of the Swinging Sixties. The city was at a fascinating intersection: while Britain's imperial power waned, the city maintained its status as a worldwide financial centre where established wealth mingled with emerging possibilities. This created an ideal setting for someone possessing Fayed's capabilities – a place where connections could be monetised and where an exotic foreigner with apparent access to Middle Eastern wealth could find a niche.

Fayed moved into a small rented flat at 60 Park Lane, Mayfair, and got to work on making it as ostentatious as he could. He also bought a white Mercedes. While he worked on his image, and the ways in which he might make his millions, his father passed away in Alexandria in 1966. None of his sons went to the funeral, nor did Dodi.

Fayed was focused on making all the connections he could and developing relationships with anyone influential or wealthy. One of these people was Abu Alwan, an Iraqi businessman living in Dubai. At the time, Dubai was a small port with a population of 50,000. Through his contact with Alwan, Fayed learned that oil was being discovered in the area, much like it had been in neighbouring Abu Dhabi. He wanted to be involved, so when he learned that Sheikh Rashid bin Saeed Al Maktoum would be visiting London with Al Tajir, a good friend of Alwan,

Fayed seized his moment. He persuaded Alwan to organise a meeting, and Fayed befriended Tajir when he came on his visit; organising parties for him filled with beautiful women, and driving him around town.

It wasn't long after Tajir's visit to London that Maktoum began to make plans for the recovery of the new oil. He instructed Tajir to find companies who could build a harbour to make this possible. Tajir mentioned this task to Fayed, who immediately threw his hat into the ring, offering grand assurances that this was something he was experienced in and could do with ease. Tajir persuaded Maktoum that Fayed was the right person for the job, and Fayed headed for Dubai to make his millions.

DUBAI

In 1968 he set up a company called International Marine Services, through which he introduced several British construction firms to Sheikh Rashid bin Saeed Al Maktoum, the ruler of Dubai and one of the founding figures of the United Arab Emirates (UAE). The construction firms helped in Maktoum's modernisation efforts.

SHEENAGH

Sheenagh was twenty-five and working in a bank in Dubai when she first encountered Fayed. At first his visits to the bank seemed innocuous – just another wealthy customer conducting business. But Fayed's appearances at her counter became more frequent, more deliberate. He began asking about her life, her past, her ambitions. She told him she had relocated to Dubai with her husband, who had taken a construction job. The questions seemed friendly, even flattering. When he offered to discuss a potential job opportunity, it felt like recognition of her business capabilities, and the professional relationship they had developed.

Sheenagh went to Fayed's private office to discuss the potential job opportunity with him in more detail. She sat across the desk from him and felt a flutter of excitement about the possibilities – this could be a new career path opening before her. Dubai was a growing country, with a bright future. By working for this wealthy man, who was in the lucrative oil business, she would be in the centre of it all.

Then Fayed stood up.

He circled the desk slowly, deliberately. He moved behind her chair.

'As I turned, the hands came over my shoulders. His hands were everywhere,' she recalls, the memory still vivid after nearly five decades.

What followed was a sexual assault. He tried to grab at her clothing and touch her breasts. When Sheenagh tried to leave, he positioned himself between her and freedom, blocking the door with his body. In desperation she slapped him – an act of self-preservation that finally created enough space for her to escape. But as she fled, his words followed her: 'You may come to regret that.'

It wasn't an idle threat. Fayed became a shadow in her life, materialising with disturbing regularity – at her workplace, at the supermarket, in the street, at her social club. Each time, he would remind her of his warning.

'The threat was there all the time,' she says, the weight of those years evident in her voice.

'On one occasion he said, "I warned you you'd regret it. Have you noticed that I'm always there?"'

This pattern of stalking and intimidation was repeated approximately twenty times. During some of these encounters, he'd follow her and assault her again, groping her body with the same entitlement he'd displayed in his office. 'I kept praying that somebody else would actually see this happen,' she says, 'thinking if somebody else sees it happen it's real and somebody will do something.'

Fayed's belief that if he wanted something he could have it, whether it was women, business deals or a major British department store was deeply ingrained by this stage. This attitude appeared to be serving him well: his business empire in Dubai was expanding. His construction projects, including the city's harbour, were building his fortune and cementing his influence, making him seem untouchable. As

Fayed's power grew, Sheenagh started to feel as if his hold over her was inescapable. Then, in 1995, the Dubai government shut down one of his companies – Dubai Trade and Trust Co. – accusing him of violating foreign ownership laws. Suddenly his time in Dubai was up, and he left.

Sheelagh described herself as being able to 'breathe freely again' once she realised he had gone.

Today Sheenagh's predominant emotion is anger – not just at what happened, but at her own silence. Like many women who would become entangled with Fayed, she wonders whether speaking out sooner might have protected others from similar experiences. She has expressed regret at not reporting her experiences to the authorities before Fayed's death.

When the recent allegations against Fayed made headlines, memories she had tried to bury for forty-seven years came rushing back. The BBC documentary about Fayed's abuse prompted her to come forward. Waiving her right to anonymity, she contacted journalists with a realisation that chilled her. 'I was hearing dates, but what happened to me was before that. I was before that,' she told them, her voice carrying the weight of a terrible question: 'Was I the start of it all? Was I the first victim?'

BRUNEI

In the same year as Fayed worked in Dubai, he became an adviser to Omar Ali Saifuddien III, the Sultan of Brunei, someone who would become extremely useful to him when he came to purchase Harrods years later. Fayed also founded his own shipping company, Genavco, and an organisation called the Middle East Navigation Company, through which he began ferrying Muslims to Saudi Arabia on their pilgrimage to Mecca. He described himself as a shipping broker and began carving a reputation as a flamboyant and successful tycoon.

He claimed to be the son of 'an old established Egyptian family', a self-invention that was not merely opportunistic but one born of a kind of psychological necessity.

Fayed's self-reinvention was a classic case of what psychologists call 'compensatory identity' – an exaggerated persona designed to gain acceptance in a foreign culture.

On Fayed's trips back to London he began establishing himself in the city's business circles and proceeded to cultivate British high society. He joined prestigious clubs, threw lavish parties and accrued an almost encyclopaedic knowledge of the British aristocracy and its customs. He studied the mannerisms, speech patterns and social codes of the upper classes, although his attempts at reproducing these often resulted in a kind of grotesque parody that amused the very people he was seeking to impress.

It was during this period that he began styling himself as 'Mohamed Al-Fayed', adding the aristocratic-sounding 'Al' prefix to his surname to enhance his perceived status and suggest noble Arab heritage. This small but significant alteration to his name symbolised his ongoing project of self-invention. And, all the time, he was making extraordinary amounts of money.

When studying Fayed it can be difficult to understand exactly what he did to become so wealthy. He appears to have arrived in countries, befriended the rich and powerful, made a load of money, caused a scandal of some kind and then left, his wealth growing with every step on his journey. But how did he do it? How *did* he make so much?

In Dubai he made his money by positioning himself as the essential middleman – the bridge between Western business interests and Arab wealth. He understood that his value lay not in what he could build or create, but in whom he knew and how he could connect parties who couldn't easily connect themselves. He cultivated relationships with an almost obsessive intensity, mapping out the contours of power and influence with the precision of a cartographer.

It's hard to give Fayed credit for much, now we've become aware of how evil he was, but he seems to have been remarkably good at making rich and powerful contacts, introducing those people to others who were equally rich and powerful and benefiting financially from any projects that went ahead between them. His skills in oiling the wheels of business were quite remarkable.

However, in a singularly Shakespearean way, Fayed carried within him the seeds of his own destruction. Just as Macbeth's ambition or Othello's jealousy led them to ruin, Fayed's hubris and disregard for rules inevitably sabotaged his carefully constructed networks. At the very moments when success seemed most assured, the fundamental flaws in his character would emerge, unravelling months and years of meticulous social engineering and ruining everything.

This time he wrecked his relationship with the Dubai hierarchy through arguments over money, and by failing to comply with government regulations. He was effectively banned from Dubai, so he fled, but he'd made a great deal of money through his business dealings in the country, enough to buy the forty flats adjacent to his own in Park Lane. He gave the most sumptuous of the apartments to his brothers and his son Dodi, who was now twenty years old, the other flats being rented out to provide further income.

Through the early part of his career, Fayed made money through contacts and knowing the right people to make things happen. As has been discussed, he was very much a middle-man, eager to throw himself into anything that might earn him money, but free to flee whenever things became difficult. He had no 'skin in the game' – no personal investment in the project that prevented him from leaving.

But he made a shift in the 1970s, moving into property acquisitions. In 1972 he bought Balnagown Castle in the Scottish Highlands, set in 65,000 acres. Next it was Barrow Green Court, near Oxted in Surrey. He bought this mansion, which sits on a large estate covering approximately 100 acres, as one of his primary residences in the United Kingdom.

RITZ HOTEL

Next he made a big splash, buying the Ritz Hotel in Paris with his brother Ali in 1979. When he took over, the hotel needed significant renovations – leaky pipes were torn out, the antiquated heating system replaced and every room redecorated. The renovation of the Ritz became Fayed's first opportunity to express his aesthetic sensibilities on a grand scale, and the results were revealing.

Where the hotel had once exemplified understated French elegance, Fayed's vision emphasised opulence and ostentation: gold taps, light switches and fittings, ornate furnishings and a kind of palatial grandeur that owed much more to his Egyptian heritage than to the Ritz's history or location. Tasteful luxury was suffocated beneath layers of gilt, crystal and exaggerated bling.

He told *Vanity Fair* magazine: 'When I bought the Ritz, I had in mind to refurbish the hotel in César Ritz's image – to do things here that would excite me and at the same time make Monsieur Ritz proud of his place if he were to see it today. It took us years, but I'm sure we brought a smile to Monsieur Ritz's face. It was a joyful experience.'

So, what had once been elegant Belle Époque splendour was transformed into a garish showcase of wealth – all glittering chandeliers, overstuffed furniture and gold-plated everything – as though Fayed believed that true opulence could be measured by how thoroughly one could banish subtlety from a space.

Fayed also installed an underground swimming pool, a culinary school and a nightclub for the Ritz clientele, 'people who care for nothing but the best', as he character-ised them. It was less about taste and more about unmistakable displays of affluence, the same philosophy that would later inform his transformation of Harrods.

HARRODS

In 1985, six years after acquiring the Ritz, Fayed made his most notorious move: he bought Harrods. He didn't have the finance, the connections or the reputation to do this, but he knew people with money and he knew how to exploit them.

The story begins with Fayed's rather complex relation-ship with Roland 'Tiny' Rowland, a businessman who owned Lonrho (London and Rhodesian Mining Company). Like Fayed, Rowland was an outsider who was keen to make inroads into British high society. He was disliked by politicians and the elite in London because he was thought to use aggressive, sometimes controversial, acquisition strategies. The South African's business methods were considered ruthless and unorthodox by the gentlemanly standards of the British commercial world. In 1973 Prime Minister Edward Heath described Rowland's business practices as 'the unacceptable face of capitalism', following a corporate governance scandal at Lonrho. This label stuck with him throughout his career.

These traits – being an outsider and employing aggressive business techniques – naturally drew Fayed to him and the two men met to discuss business. Rowland was trying to take over the House of Fraser group at the time, a move that would bring Harrods, the legendary Knightsbridge department store, into his ownership.

Despite his reputation, Rowland possessed a shrewd business intellect. He'd transformed Lonrho from a small enterprise into a conglomerate with interests ranging from mining to newspapers, hotels to car dealerships. For years he'd set his sights on a single prize that would cement his place in British commerce: Harrods, the jewel in the crown of the House of Fraser group.

Rowland had been acquiring shares in House of Fraser throughout the early 1980s, but his efforts to buy Harrods had been repeatedly thwarted by regulatory hurdles. The Monopolies and Mergers Commission had blocked his takeover attempts, citing concerns about market concentration. Frustrated but not defeated, Rowland continued his pursuit, looking for creative ways to overcome these obstacles. It was against this backdrop that Fayed entered the ring.

In 1984 Fayed approached Rowland with what seemed like a mutually beneficial proposition, the Egyptian could help Rowland finally secure House of Fraser. With his connections to Middle Eastern wealth and lower profile with British regulators, Fayed suggested he could acquire some shares and later transfer them to Lonrho, circumventing the regulatory hurdles that had frustrated Rowland.

This was a great idea from Rowland's point of view. Here was someone with apparent access to Gulf money who seemed content to play a supporting role in his grand ambition. They began to coordinate their efforts, or so Rowland believed.

What Rowland didn't realise was that he was being played in a high-stakes game of commercial chess. While appearing to work with Lonrho, Fayed was secretly hatching his own plan to seize House of Fraser by quietly accumulating shares.

In November 1984, House of Fraser's share price began to rise unexpectedly. Rowland, initially unconcerned, assumed this was part of their joint strategy. By February 1985, however, the truth became clear. Fayed, along with his brothers, launched a surprise £615 million takeover bid for the entire House of Fraser group. While Rowland had faced years of regulatory scrutiny, Fayed's bid received remarkably swift approval from Trade Secretary Norman Tebbit. No referral to the Monopolies and Mergers

Commission, no extended investigation – just a green light that left Rowland stunned. He never imagined being conned by someone he considered a friend, and he had no idea that Fayed had the money to make such an audacious bid.

There was widespread bewilderment about where Fayed had obtained the money for the acquisition. And people were right to be bewildered . . . Fayed didn't have the money.

But he knew a man who did.

He leveraged his relationship with the Sultan of Brunei to create the impression of vast financial resources. But it was only ever an impression of wealth. It was the business equivalent of smoke and mirrors.

Having cultivated the trust of Brunei's rulers since 1966 – Omar Ali Saifuddien III had abdicated in 1967 and been succeeded as sultan by his eldest son Hassanal Bolkiah – Fayed had positioned himself as an intermediary for their European business affairs. This carefully nurtured relationship meant Fayed having access to the sultan's wealth as he made acquisitions for him.

In the summer of 1984, the year before his purchase of Harrods, Fayed received several powers of attorney and written authorisations from the Sultan of Brunei to carry out tasks for him. These gave him legal access to large sums of the sultan's cash.

The Fayed brothers had £50.5 million ($69 million) on deposit in the Royal Bank of Scotland. Their bank then received a sudden transfer of hundreds of millions of dollars from Switzerland. Fayed never explained where this money came from; the bank assumed it belonged to the sultan. However, the Sultan of Brunei has since denied that he played a role in the takeover of House of Fraser plc. He issued a statement saying that he had not given money to Mohamed, Salah and Ali Fayed to help them buy it, although he acknowledged that he'd given a power of attorney to Mohamed, who bought the Dorchester Hotel on his behalf. He added that, if the power of attorney was used for something else, it was done wholly without the sultan's authority or knowledge.

With or without the sultan's knowledge the Fayed brothers had the money in their account, and their bid was pushed through without investigation. Fayed took ownership of the Queen's department store, with Rowland being on the receiving end of one of the most impertinent corporate hijackings in British business history. Rowland naturally saw it as a huge personal betrayal that demanded retribution, and launched a relentless campaign to expose the Fayeds. He used his ownership of the *Observer* newspaper, which'd he bought in 1981, to publish damaging stories about the brothers, and he lobbied government officials to scrutinise the takeover retrospectively.

His persistence eventually paid off in 1990 with the publication of the Department of Trade and Industry (DTI) report, which concluded the Fayeds had 'dishonestly misrepresented their origins, their wealth, their business interests and their resources'. This was a devastating official condemnation, although it came too late to reverse the House of Fraser acquisition.

The DTI report specifically questioned the miraculous timing of Fayed's sudden wealth, noting, 'It may be no more than coincidence that this vast increase in disposable wealth followed quickly on the admission of Mohamed to the sultan's confidence. It is, however, a very powerful coincidence.'

The bitter irony of this feud wasn't lost on observers of British business. It was a clash between two men on the fringes, each vying for dominance over the heart of the British Establishment. Rowland, for all his years of building Lonrho and his decades in Britain, remained 'the unacceptable face of capitalism'. But he'd been outmanoeuvred by an even more audacious outsider – a man who'd emerged from the slums of Alexandria to claim one of the glittering prizes of British commerce. The rivalry would continue for years, with lawsuits, counter-lawsuits and public accusations flying between the two men.

MEETING HEINI

With Harrods secured in 1985, Fayed's interest turned, briefly, away from business and to romance when he proposed to his girlfriend, Heini Wathén, a model and beauty queen thirty years his junior. The couple had met eighteen months earlier when Dodi introduced them.

Dodi had been at the Miss Finland pageant looking for models for Pierre Balmain, the French fashion designer. Wathén was knocked out of the competition at the semifinal stage, but she caught Dodi's eye. He offered her work with Balmain and introduced her to his fifty-six-year-old father. Wathén was twenty-six at the time.

Before she met Fayed, Wathén had been working as an actress and model, having been persuaded to pursue modelling by her sister. She began her career after high school and signed with an agency when she was just seventeen. There are no public records of any productions she appeared in as an actress, but a source close to the family confirmed that she did feature in several when she was young. Once she married Fayed, she worked at Harrods, then stopped working when she had her first child.

In 1986, a year after the couple's marriage, Fayed's first wife Samira Khashoggi died of a heart attack.

3

IMPERIAL WHIMS AND GOLD SPHINXES

HOW FAYED REMADE HARRODS IN HIS IMAGE

'I'm a hard person to please. I always want the
ultimate in perfection. I have always been in charge.
I am the person who has to generate the power,
the discipline, the management of our affairs
and the fantasy of the stores.'

Fayed

It had demanded a considerable amount of obfuscation, subterfuge and misrepresentation, but Fayed had done it. He had Harrods in his possession and the fun could really start. His first job was to take the rather sophisticated store that had been a commercial triumph since it opened its doors in Knightsbridge in 1849, and make wholesale changes to it.

'I was working at Harrods before Mohamed Al-Fayed arrived and the moment he walked through the door, everything changed,' said Rebecca who was twenty-one in 1985 and had been at Harrods for six months before the takeover. 'It was a very calm working life when I first arrived there. There was the "Harrods way", which meant being polite and understated. We were encouraged not to "hard sell" but make sure it was a positive, enjoyable experience for customers. I remember being told that Harrods sold itself, it was the best store in the world, we didn't need to be pushy.

'Roy Snook had been CEO for thirteen years, so we all knew what to expect, there was stability.

'When Mr Al-Fayed came, Snook was out, and everything was thrown up into the air. Fayed was there all the time, telling us to sell and pushing us to talk to customers. One time he came onto the floor as a shopper was leaving and he practically made me chase her out through the doors, trying to sell her some perfume, with him running behind me, flapping his arms around.'

Rebecca was called up to the offices, after a few months, and was asked to join the marketing team. She was told that Fayed thought she'd be better suited to marketing.

'I took it as a compliment that he'd seen potential in me, but then I saw the women arriving to work on the shop floor and they were all tall, slim and gorgeous, so I realised he didn't think I was attractive enough to be public-facing, and I was in an office with other people who, presumably, weren't the "right look" either.

'Every day was mad. At the start, he brought in design experts who knew nothing about design but were friends or sometimes just random people he'd met. They were all trying to have their say and he was overruling them. The place began to transform from a relatively quiet, understated workplace to a madhouse. We didn't know what we were doing.'

In the middle of it all was Fayed, like the Mad March Hare, jumping from one project to another, making impulsive decisions and transforming everything with a good deal more feverish enthusiasm than sensible thinking.

'He wanted everything done quickly – like yesterday,' says Rebecca. 'There was no formal planning, no thinking about branding or whatever the equivalent term would have been in the 80s, just him walking through the store and shouting instructions while we all ran behind with notebooks, writing it all down and looking at one another with confused faces.

'There were elements of working for him back then that were funny. "I want that big door painted gold. And once you've had that big door painted green, can someone do something about that wall." We'd spend the next half hour thinking – gold or green? Do what to the wall? What does he want? If you went and asked him, he'd tell you to stop fussing about the wall; there was lots of work to be done on the shop floor, so then you'd be given a pile of instructions about that. I've never worked with any boss who was so hands-on. He contradicted himself, changed his mind, accused us of not listening and was generally your worst nightmare. He was impossible to work for because he wouldn't stop to think at all.'

So were there any red flags in these early days?

'He was one big red flag, but I only realise that now. At the time we just put up with it. It was the 1980s, men were much less constrained back then. He always had his hands on your hips or was squeezing your shoulders or pinching your cheeks. He commented on what women looked like and was rude about women who weren't dressed up and made-up to the nines. He encouraged us to wear make-up, and he hung around the younger women on the sales floor, leering at them.'

Despite his best efforts to run House of Fraser himself, Fayed soon realised the magnitude of the task and brought Brian Walsh over from Australia as the new CEO. Walsh would be in charge of seventy stores, including Harrods.

When he first arrived – in 1986 – Walsh declared himself 'thrilled' with the opportunity to begin the renovations and rebranding, as he introduced himself to the staff at a series of hastily arranged meetings. Walsh and Fayed shared the view that big changes needed to be made, and that there was no place for sentimentality. He began by closing the lending library and the kennels. These were admittedly just small changes, but they'd been services that had helped Harrods stand out, bespoke offerings that other stores didn't provide. Regular Harrods customers began to express dismay at the changes taking place.

Fayed was temporarily distracted in 1986, spending time out of the country to buy Villa Windsor in the Bois de Boulogne, on the western edge of Paris. The villa was the former home of the Duke and Duchess of Windsor (Edward VIII, who abdicated the British throne in 1936, and Wallis Simpson), and appealed to Fayed because of his growing fascination with the royal family. It was in this year that he sponsored the Royal Windsor Horse Show and Windsor Park Polo Challenge Cup (sometimes also referred to as the Harrods Polo Cup) at Windsor Great Park. Prince Charles and Princess Diana were at the event in 1986, and photographs show him bursting with pride as he poses next to them.

Back at Harrods, Walsh had begun work on closing House of Fraser stores that were less profitable, and identifying which of Harrods's staff members weren't up to the job. He sold twenty stores, along with the funeral business, and began to dismiss employees from the Knightsbridge flagship.

But once Fayed was back, and overseeing things again, he began to feel that, despite his possessing absolutely no background in retail and no understanding of the market, it should be he who was running the operation.

So, Walsh found himself on a plane home, with Fayed declaring that he was now both chairman and CEO. 'I'm a hard person to please,' he said. 'I always want the ultimate in perfection. I have always been in charge. I am the person who has to generate the power, the discipline, the management of our affairs and the fantasy of the stores.'

The *Canberra Times* speculated in October 1987 that the reason for Walsh's departure was a clash of personalities. Essentially, Walsh found it hard to accept Fayed's hands-on style of management. What later emerged was that the two men had completely different ideas about what the store should look like. Fayed wanted everything to appear busy, opulent and shiny, whereas Walsh liked a sleeker, more modern look. One of the incidents that had resulted in a falling out between the two men was when Fayed hung bunches of bananas from a chandelier. Walsh thought he was joking and moved to take them down.

'No joking,' replied Fayed. 'This is how to run an exclusive business.'

Walsh wasn't so sure.

Fayed spent a fortune on renovating Harrods in his own image. The exact amount isn't clear, but estimates – from looking back at accounts and reports from the time – suggest it to have been between £400 million and £500 million (not adjusted for inflation), around two-thirds of the initial purchase price.

One of the most significant changes Fayed made was the installation of the Egyptian escalator in the early 1990s. Formally known as the 'Egyptian Hall and Escalator', it featured ornate hieroglyphics, gilded pharaonic statues and sphinx sculptures, and wasn't a universally loved addition. The art critic Brian Sewell was particularly scathing, calling it 'a vulgar facade' and 'Tutankhamun's tomb reimagined by Cecil B. DeMille'. He further commented that it represented 'the worst kind of pastiche – neither authentic Egyptian nor good design'. Architectural critic Jonathan Glancey also offered his opinion, describing it as 'an exercise in pharaonic kitsch that would make even Liberace blush', adding that it was 'symptomatic of the cultural collision between old-money British restraint and new-money exuberance'.

At the bottom of the Egyptian escalator on the ground floor was the Egyptian Room, in which a mix of genuine antiquities from Fayed's personal collection sat alongside high-quality replicas. These included small statues, scarabs, amulets and ceremonial items in display cases, as well as a sphinx and busts of Nefertiti and Tutankhamun. Most controversially, the room included depictions of Fayed himself in pharaonic pose and dress.

Sociologists have identified what they call 'status inconsistency', the psychological effects of achieving high economic status without corresponding social acceptance. Research shows that individuals in this position often exhibit psychological distress and compensatory behaviours, including displays of excessive wealth, attempts to buy influence and the exploitation of others. Fayed's behaviour as Harrods owner seems to fit neatly into this category.

Other changes that Fayed initiated were to do with emphasising the exclusivity and status of the store. He created a Harrods Gold Card for VIP customers, an invitation-only card designed to be a status symbol. Fayed watched over the Gold Card list, occasionally adding or removing people as they fell in and out of his favour. Cardholders were offered personal shoppers, after-hours shopping, home delivery and invitations to exclusive events. The programme proved particularly appealing to wealthy international visitors – especially from the Middle East, Russia and Asia, who valued both the practical benefits and the status conferred – and was one of Fayed's more successful innovations at Harrods. It demonstrated his understanding of luxury retail psychology and the value of exclusivity. When Qatar Holdings bought Harrods in 2010, they maintained and expanded the loyalty programme, which suggested it had genuine business value beyond Fayed's personal whims.

Fayed also introduced a helicopter service for his wealthiest customers. It was launched in the late 1980s, offering transfers between Harrods and major London airports as well as private airfields. The helicopters' livery was the distinctive Harrods green and gold, and featured the store's logo and Fayed's coat of arms, making them highly recognisable when flying over London.

While Harrods itself didn't have a helipad due to urban planning restrictions, the helicopter transportation operated from designated helipads nearby, including one at Battersea. This amenity included luxury cars to and from the helipads, with Harrods-branded vehicles meeting customers and handling their shopping packages. In a particularly extravagant touch, customers could shop via catalogue while in transit, with purchases ready for them upon arrival at the store. This option was available primarily to Harrods Gold Card holders.

But the helicopter transport wasn't cheap: a one-way transfer between Battersea Heliport and Heathrow or Gatwick reportedly cost between £2,000 to £3,000. For bespoke journeys to private estates or other locations, prices were significantly higher, starting at around £5,000. Frequent users were able to buy package deals or membership options that provided a certain number of flights annually, with prices reportedly starting at £25,000 to £30,000 per year. For high-value customers (those spending millions at Harrods annually), complimentary helicopter transfers were offered as part of their VIP treatment.

This need to create an exclusive, sophisticated shopping environment was central to Fayed's refurbishment of Harrods. He cared less about what it cost to provide exclusive amenities than he did about how these luxurious offerings reflected on him.

The new Egyptian escalator cost between £30 million and £40 million; the updating of the old accounting system, which now linked every cash till to a central computer, set him back about £50 million; while the renovation of the food halls came to around £25 million. The security system that he would go on to use and abuse for his own benefit is thought to have commanded a price tag of around £20 million; the Diana and Dodi memorial, including the 'Innocent Victims' statue, added in 1997, reportedly came in at around £3 million; and the Harrods helicopter service, including the purchase and branding of helicopters, represented an investment of approximately £15 million. On top of all this, Fayed maintained an annual renovation budget that reportedly ranged between £10 million to £20 million for ongoing updates and maintenance. Over a span of twenty-five years, that was going to add up, but he wanted his store to scream 'opulence' and no cost was too high for that.

Soon after taking over the store, he imposed an official dress code for shoppers, with items such as high-cut shorts, flip-flops, cycling shorts and other casual wear prohibited. It was largely down to security officers on the door to enforce this dress code, but Fayed sometimes stepped in himself, particularly in the early years of his ownership.

'I can definitely remember him standing near entrances, slightly out of view, watching customers entering the store,' says Rebecca. 'If someone was dressed in clothes he thought were too scruffy, he'd jump out and bar them from entering. Sometimes the person was scruffy, but not actually breaking any of the rules on Fayed's list, but he'd just decide he didn't want them in the store, and the security guard would be in trouble for letting them in. It was as if the security guards were supposed to be able to read Fayed's mind. Of course it worked the other way round too – people who broke the dress code were allowed in if they were wealthy customers, pretty girls or those Fayed liked.'

There were accusations that Fayed was using the dress code as a pretext for racial or class-based discrimination, with claims that white or wealthy shoppers were admitted while similarly clad customers from ethnic minorities were turned away. There were also multiple incidents involving tourists who'd travelled to London specifically to visit Harrods, only to be turned away at the door, resulting in complaints to the English Tourist Board.

4

LOYALTY THROUGH FEAR

BUILDING THE SECURITY MACHINE

'You will protect me from bullets. You will throw
yourself in front of them.'

Fayed, addressing his newly formed security team

LOYALTY
THROUGH FEAR

When Fayed first arrived at Harrods and posed theatrically outside the doors, he was accompanied by two bodyguards. Mick Lee and Brian Dodd represented the entirety of his personal security detail. Two ordinary men in unremarkable suits watching everything while maintaining a calculated distance from their prickly employer. It was a woefully inadequate shield for a man who had cultivated such a spectacular collection of enemies over the previous decade.

Behind him stretched a wake of broken promises, financial deceptions and powerful adversaries spanning continents. From vengeful business partners to government officials left holding worthless IOUs, Fayed's rise had been built on a foundation of burned bridges. Most chilling of all were the rumours that Papa Doc's notorious Tonton Macoute – Haiti's feared death squad who had earned their name from the Creole bogeyman who kidnapped children in the night – had added Fayed to their list of unfinished business.

He needed a better security set-up, so Mick Lee was summoned to his office and asked how many bodyguards would be required for twenty-four-hour-a-day security. Lee suggested that around thirty extra officers would be necessary. He assumed Fayed would baulk at such a high number and the related expenses, but the chairman didn't seem bothered at all. He was far more interested in public displays of success and wealth than he was in actual wealth.

Mark Rowe, editor of *Professional Security Magazine*, says this is an extremely unusual stance, and that parting with money for security, however wealthy the person is, is always very difficult for a retailer to justify. 'The bugbear is always that any spend on security anywhere is money off the bottom line. Will the expense of hiring twenty-four-hour-a-day security be recoverable in terms of identifying shoplifters? Do we lose so much through shoplifting that this level of security is needed?'

But Fayed wasn't interested in that. The bottom line was important, but nowhere near as glamorous or as exciting as the image of him being surrounded by security personnel. He wanted a ring of steel, and he wanted people to be aware of that ring; so that's what Lee set out to provide, and a team of twenty-four was initially recruited, mainly from the armed forces.

Fayed ensured that the first tranche of security guards was kept onside by pushing thousands of pounds towards them. Whenever they did anything that appealed to him, they were offered brown envelopes stuffed with notes. He bought their loyalty, but he always reminded them that the money was to keep them quiet and that if they took it, they'd made a pact with him to always do as he asked and never to talk publicly about what they'd witnessed.

'It didn't feel like that was too much of a stretch. Those of us who'd been in the army knew all about following orders and the importance of keeping your mouth shut. We happily agreed to those conditions because they were exactly what we were used to,' said 'Biggie', one of the security guards recruited in that first group.

Dr Jerry Hart has wide-ranging experience of working with individuals and companies on their security set-ups, and he says there are three reasons why people opt for security guards: for personal protection, to keep the company safe and to make themselves look important.

While Fayed may have felt he needed security for his own safety, it's undeniable that this third factor played a key role in his decision to surround himself with bodyguards from the armed forces. He wanted the men – his guards were all male – to look the part, and he'd comment on the size of the bigger men and request the removal of guys who didn't look sufficiently intimidating. He liked to be feared, to feel powerful. He wanted people to know when he was in town. He wanted to be visible, but untouchable.

'Wealthy people like to be surrounded by guys in black with sunglasses on,' says Hart. 'They like huge security officers to create a feeling of power and intimidation. They feel like their security team are the visible manifestation of the power they have. It absolutely suits Fayed's personality that he would have done this. There's one problem with creating a ring of steel around you, though. It isolates you. It's designed to separate you from the crowd and make you stand out, which it does, but it also insulates you from the reality of what's going on around. That can cause problems when you're the leader of a big organisation.'

There's no question that an imposing security detail appealed to Fayed's ego, but there was more to it than that. His desire for security officers was like an arrow through time, linking the poor young boy growing up in Alexandria with the rich and successful middle-aged man running the most famous department store in the world.

The well-groomed British officers he'd watched strolling through his home city surrounded by security guards had seemed so superior – a quality that he saw in himself. Now he would surround himself with imposing bodyguards.

Once Fayed had his first security team in place, he became obsessed with strengthening it. Mick Lee's team were good, but could they be better? He called Lord Bramall, former chief of the defence staff and a man of great standing, and asked him for advice. Bramall had taken part in the D-Day landings and became Lord Lieutenant of Greater London after retiring from the army in 1985 (the year that Fayed bought Harrods); he was subsequently created a life peer and invested as a Knight of the Garter.

One suspects that he might have had more pressing things to do than attend to the demands of the Harrods chairman, but he took Fayed's call and answered his questions. He told him that Jonathan Heywood, a former major in the Grenadier Guards, was just the man to help him sort out his security. Heywood was summoned to Knightsbridge to meet Fayed but was an immediate disappointment. He was dressed far too casually for the chairman's tastes, in an anorak and jeans. 'I was there when he turned up. I took one look at him and thought, "Well, this isn't going to go down very well,"' says Biggie. 'The boss liked people to look smart and professional. He particularly wanted his security team to look fierce and intimidating. It's probably one of the reasons he was so attracted to soldiers. They'd show up with shiny shoes and perfectly ironed trousers; he loved all that shit.'

Presumably Fayed expected a former major in the Grenadier Guards to look like an on-duty guard. Instead, Heywood arrived dressed like a student after a big night out. But Heywood's rhetorical skills must have been more impressive than his sartorial prowess because he was duly appointed, soon taking the reins and scrutinising the security operation that was in place.

Heywood was deeply unimpressed by what he saw and demanded the immediate removal of Lee, who'd turned the security operation at Harrods into his own private fiefdom. Lee was given £25k and shown the door. There was a new man in town. Heywood proved to be more efficient and professional than his predecessors, and he worked quickly to dismantle the self-serving system in operation. Indeed, after he'd looked through the list of security staff on the payroll, he deemed that most of them would have to go.

Biggie survived this 'night of the long knives', along with, he thinks, eight other people. Everyone else was fired. 'Those of us who were kept on were told that our salaries would be £19,500. This was a decent pay at the time, to be fair. It was more than security guards were getting elsewhere. I was pleased. It felt like a real achievement to have been kept on when so many had been sacked.'

But things didn't go well for long. Fayed became very impatient with Heywood. 'After a while you could sense the frustration,' recalls Biggie. 'I guess it's because Heywood was being very particular and trying to do things properly, and Fayed wasn't interested in things being done properly – he was a showman. When he told Fayed to wear an armoured vest, Fayed refused, and said, "I don't need it – you will protect me from bullets. You will throw yourself in front of them."

'There was the same reaction to Fayed having security in the car with him – he wanted to be in the car on his own, with his bodyguards like outriders. It was madness . . . how were we supposed to keep him safe? We'd be in a separate car, following his car, and he'd usually say, "Follow me" but not tell us where he was going. It was like he was more worried about the bodyguards he'd employed than any outside force. Why not tell us where he was going? He kept us at arms' length, as he did everyone.

'One thing we always laughed about was that he had these clip-on ties so that if someone grabbed him by the tie he couldn't be strangled, and he seemed to think these were going to be his saviour. He was forever pulling at the tie to show me how it wouldn't strangle him.

'There must have been a part of him that was genuinely worried about his safety. He'd upset a lot of people by this stage, some real tough guys. He'd crossed Papa Doc Duvalier, for God's sake. I don't think a clip-on tie was going to help him if a pile of gun-toting outlaws from Haiti turned up.

'Things got worse and worse. It felt like there was one problem after another, and Heywood was being told about everything that Fayed didn't like in front of us all. It undermined Heywood's authority, so he was too scared to suggest anything. I didn't get on with Heywood – he'd sacked all my friends – but I did feel sorry for him. He was trying to do everything right, when it had been a shambles before.'

The mistake Heywood made was thinking that Fayed wanted a genuine close-protection team, whereas the Harrods chairman was interested in a display of dominance. Subtlety didn't interest him in the least. An undetectable security presence was no fun at all for the King of Bling. His staff recruitment was all about appearance and aggressive messaging.

While trying to organise his security guards, and meddling endlessly in the way they operated, he was also engaged in the ongoing battle with 'Tiny' Rowland, his business adversary and the man whom he'd duped to acquire Harrods. Rowland was trying to trip him up at every stage, persuading the government to investigate the veracity of all the claims he'd made about his wealth before acquiring Harrods and doing all he could to expose Fayed as the crook Rowland knew him to be.

Fayed discovered that Rowland had employed former police officers as part of his team and that they'd been following him and taping his calls. Most clear-minded people might have considered this an assault on their privacy. Not Fayed. He thought it a fine idea and concluded that he needed former police officers on his staff, particularly those with the skills to perform covert operations. Thus began Fayed's close links with members of the police, some of whom would offer him information and protection throughout his life.

Fayed organised a meeting with Sir David McNee, a former commissioner of the Metropolitan Police, who recommended a man called John Macnamara as a possible head of security. There were backhanders to McNee for his help, and he was brought on as an advisor and paid handsomely to boost his pension.

Macnamara struck Fayed as a good man because he'd be a match for Kenneth Etheridge, the former detective chief superintendent who was on Rowland's books. Macnamara came with a good reputation. He'd spent twenty-eight years in the police and had an unblemished track record, in his later years he was deputy head of the Scotland Yard Fraud Squad. He was well known and highly respected.

In reality, however, Macnamara was a nasty bully. His nickname was 'Mac the Knife' and he delighted in the position of supreme power offered by Fayed. There were no depths to which this new employee would not sink.

As soon as Macnamara arrived at Harrods he began to add to the small army of security staff that existed. Many of those he brought on were ex-policemen. Under his leadership, these men were given licence to act with impunity: threatening employees and bugging phones.

When Fayed said he wanted to know exactly what was going on in the store, and what was being said, Macnamara acted quickly, and recording devices were attached to telephones and monitoring video cameras were installed.

In the basement there was a wall of screens being watched by security officers. Around forty screens flickered day and night, supplying Macnamara and his team with information from every last corner of the store.

'There was a seriousness to the basement, and the guys looked at the screens as if their lives depended on it,' recalls Biggie. 'But they also realised that many of the questions Macnamara asked were about females who had caught Fayed's eye, so there was also a lot of sniggering as they watched women in changing rooms and toilets.' This Rabelaisian response was typical of life behind the scenes – the seriousness of ensuring there were sophisticated responses to every question posed by Macnamara and Fayed, coupled with a bawdiness that reflected the culture of the organisation. And everything they did was untroubled by thoughts of decency or common sense. Cameras in the ladies' toilets? Fine! Cameras in the public changing rooms? No problem! Fayed wanting to know exactly where an attractive teenager was at any stage. Fine! Fayed wanting the teenager to be followed. No problem!

Seven years after his arrival, Macnamara was promoted to become head of security.

He retained good relationships with those he had worked with in the Met, and cemented the relationships by dishing out hampers and cash inducements to several police officers, and paying them to help him. With the police on his side he was able to access the police computer, have misbehaving staff members falsely arrested, and make sure that any allegations about Fayed were dropped at the first stage.

'There were cameras all over the building, even in the public areas,' says Biggie. 'Fayed was watching the staff, but lots of customers were also seen on screen. The cameras were in the staff ladies' toilets because he suspected that women would gather in there to chat and he needed to know what they were saying. They were also in locker rooms and changing rooms. Also – and people don't talk about this – there were cameras right up to the entrance and slightly inside the changing rooms used by Harrods customers, which meant if you were in a Harrods changing room during the Fayed era, there was a good chance that he was watching you.'

'I had a run-in with a business leader from a Latin American country once,' says Hart. 'He'd messed with the CCTV system to watch people in his store. He didn't think it was a problem; he thought he had the right to do that. The problem in Latin America is that there is not always a legal recourse in the same way as here, but if Fayed had bought the police, as is claimed, then it would be impossible to catch him. There's no legal recourse, so it becomes lawless.

'Remember, in this country, the police have discretionary powers, not codified laws, so the police might say, "Don't do it again" and move, or they might double-down and arrest or charge you. They have the right to do that; the right to judge a situation. If they were being paid by Fayed, or understood that others were, they might well fob complainants off.'

So Fayed had his army of protection officers who acted with impunity, searching out 'wrongdoers' or anyone whose face didn't fit. It seems that the modern management adage 'try to catch people doing something good' in order to inspire them and value them wasn't part of Fayed's management strategy. The opposite, in fact, was true. It was made clear to employees that everything they said and did was being captured on film and he was looking out for trouble.

And just to emphasise this, the films in the cameras were replaced in front of employees and cameras were moved around frequently, so staff never knew where cameras were. This meant, in effect, that cameras were everywhere. Working at Harrods was like living in *The Truman Show*. Nothing went unnoticed in the building.

And although a primary job of the security team was to record everything and report back to Fayed on all movements or conversations that might interest or amuse him, they too were being monitored. In this weird dystopian world, the monsters were eating themselves and each other.

5

POWERFUL KNOWLEDGE

WHAT THATCHER AND THE REAGANS KNEW

'Yes, you will. You will sleep with me tonight.'

Fayed to Melissa Price

Fayed had owned Harrods for a year and was peacocking his way around London, attending the swankiest parties, mixing with the most beautiful people and eating the finest food. Harrods was being transformed into the store of his dreams, he was reunited with his son Dodi in London and he felt invincible.

It was 1986, the year when everything he touched turned to gold and he started to feel indestructible. He could do anything he wanted, be anything he wanted and own anyone he wanted. He had the beautiful mansion in the country, forty flats in Mayfair, a villa in Paris and a wonderful castle in Scotland. He owned the House of Fraser group and he owned the Ritz in Paris. What Fayed desired, Fayed got.

As befitted his new position in society, he was invited to the finest parties, including those held by the US ambassador to the UK at Winfield House, the ambassador's official residence, set in more than twelve acres of Regent's Park in central London. At one of these parties he met a teenage girl called Melissa Price.

Price had come to live in London three years earlier, in 1983. It was a time of economic hardship and industrial decline. Recession, high unemployment rates after widespread job losses in manufacturing, coupled with Cold War tensions and the activities of the IRA gave people a sense of unease.

One favourable aspect, though, was the mutual admiration and trust that had grown between Margaret Thatcher and Ronald Reagan. Since Reagan's election victory in 1981, they had built a strong bond, a 'special relationship', which strengthened the Anglo-American alliance at a volatile time. It was seen as a hugely positive aspect of 1980s politics.

'There was the unification of Germany in the 1980s, as well as the dissolution of the Soviet Union. World politics was changing shape, and Europe was beginning to look very different. The powerful bond built up between the USA and the UK over the decade was vitally important,' says Jack Straw, an MP in the 80s, who would go on to become Home Secretary.

In 1983, however, came a moment of unease between the two leaders. Thatcher had not been notified before the United States invasion of Grenada, and many British elected officials opposed the idea of basing American cruise missiles in Britain. Meetings were called, phone calls took place, and a flurry of Downing Street and White House officials worked to align the two leaders.

It was into all this that Charles H. Price II was thrown, as the newly appointed US ambassador to the Court of St James's. Price was an experienced ambassador, promoted from his posting in Belgium to become his country's envoy to the UK in November 1983. It is Price who is credited with easing the pressure and rebuilding that crucial relationship. He threw himself into all the big battles of the day, including talks between the British and the IRA, and when Pan Am Flight 103 was brought down by a terrorist bomb over Lockerbie, killing all 259 people aboard, Price and his wife were at the scene within hours.

He is regarded as one of the most effective ambassadors of his generation, a man with a booming laugh, dubbed 'The Bear' by friends because of his penchant for hugging people at social events. *The Times* described him as 'the most energetic, engaging and popular American ambassador'.

He was joined in his move to London by his wife Carol and his children, including his sixteen-year-old daughter Melissa, who threw herself into life in London, making new friends and attending banquets and drinks parties with her family, as part of her father's ambassadorial role. She began studying History of Art at the London Fine Arts school and enjoyed life.

And so to the dinner party, organised at Winfield House, with Melissa in attendance. There was a mixed group for the evening, a dozen leading figures from business, politics and retail, including Fayed, who was seated on Melissa's right-hand side. It was a meeting that would change the course of her life.

They chatted through the evening, Melissa feeling that he was a perfectly acceptable dinner companion, even charming at times, but she didn't think any more of it until Fayed got in touch afterwards and offered Melissa a job at his offices in Park Lane. He said that because she was studying Fine Art, and had a good eye, he'd like her to help him to buy antiques and update his decor. She says the role he offered was vague, and he didn't seem to know what he wanted. But she figured that's why he wanted her to get involved because he didn't have a clue about art or interior design.

She considered the offer, talked it over with her parents, and decided that it would be good fun, so she accepted.

'He gave me drawings and plans of his homes and apartments for which he wanted me to buy furnishings. It never occurred to me that he had any other motives in providing me a job,' Melissa told the *Mail on Sunday* newspaper. It wouldn't be long, however, before he began showering her with cash and gifts, which she found strange and a little oppressive. 'He was offended when I tried to refuse them and so I stashed them in a drawer.'

One day in September 1986, while at his office, he asked her whether she had her passport with her. He suggested they go to Paris for the day as he'd like her to take a look at his apartment on the Champs-Élysées and advise on pieces of art that he might purchase. Once across the Channel they went briefly to his apartment, then they went to the Paris Ritz, where they were to have a working dinner. Melissa assumed this was to discuss art and the way his apartment had been decorated. But she soon became concerned – this business dinner was arranged at a banquette in a dark corner of the restaurant, 'somewhere you'd sit on a date, not with your teenage work assistant,' she says.

During dinner he made his move. Unconcerned, it seems, about the consequences of messing around with the daughter of a US ambassador, he put his hands under her skirt and rubbed her legs, telling her, 'You're getting into my bed tonight.' Despite Melissa insisting that this wouldn't be happening, he was resolute. 'Yes, you will. You will sleep with me tonight.'

When she went to her hotel room that evening, the electricity had been switched off. 'The lights went out as my punishment for not sleeping with him. I went looking for a phone to call London to speak to my parents, but one of Fayed's security guards followed me as soon as I left my room.' Fayed had also taken her diplomatic passport and refused to return it.

'I felt like his prisoner in a foreign country with no means of escape,' she recalls.

He didn't attempt to come into her bed that evening, but the next morning she saw him having breakfast in his apartment with a very young French girl, 'no older than fifteen'.

Fayed told her that his plans had changed and that instead of staying in Paris to discuss his decor, they would go to inspect his beachside house in Saint-Tropez. Once there, he suggested a trip on his yacht, moored nearby. He claimed that her father had been contacted and approved the trip, and that he was expecting her back the following day. He still refused to return her passport, so she had no choice but to accompany him. Once she was on the yacht, she was stuck. She couldn't escape, and he knew it.

When she thinks back to the evening now, she remembers the sound of Middle Eastern music playing and the speed with which Fayed's mind turned to sex, demanding that she sleep with him. The more Melissa resisted, the more demanding he became. She's sure that the more she resisted, the more excited he became.

He wore a kaftan and battled during dinner to persuade her to sleep with him in what she describes as 'an enclosed, airless, tastelessly decorated dining room'. It's a vile image. She says she felt 'verbally raped' as he ran through, in great detail, exactly what he wanted to do to her.

'I just wanted to get off the boat. I felt sick, I needed some air. I left the dinner table to go to the deck and Fayed followed me. I saw how far out we were from land. I was stuck on this boat with a sick, vile man nearly the same age as my father. Fayed told everyone on deck to go away. This was the first time I'd felt in true danger. I was shaking.'

Melissa reminded Fayed who her father was and told him that he'd be in a great deal of trouble if he were to do anything to her. His response was to boast that he was richer and more powerful than her father would ever be.

Fayed genuinely believed that he was the most powerful man in the world and thought nothing of demeaning girls' fathers in front of them. When Fayed attacked Bianca Gascoigne, daughter of England footballer Paul Gascoigne, in 2004, he repeatedly told her that her father was a 'bad father', and made comments about his mental health and addiction problems.

With Melissa, he emphasised how much more money he had than her father as he ran through the disgusting things he wished to do to her. This 'verbal rape' soon turned to physical violence as Fayed became aggressive and pushed himself against the teenager, clutching her so tightly it hurt. She had no way of moving and could hardly breathe as he squeezed her, constricting her arms and chest.

He continued telling her what he wanted to do to her, some of the things so utterly depraved that she doesn't want to talk about them even now, decades after the incident. 'It felt like he was trying to rape me through my clothes. At the same time, he was telling me to lie down on the deck. I remember wanting to cry but stopped myself, thinking Fayed might like that.'

She screamed out, hoping that someone would come to her aid, but there was no sign of the many security officers who'd been a constant presence until Fayed had shooed them away. She says she shouted and screamed as loud as she could, and she knows the staff on the yacht would have heard her.

As panic set in and she was unable to fight him off – he had her arms pinned by her side as he pushed himself against her – she bit down hard on his arm. He shouted and staff came rushing to his aid. She'd been screaming for ten minutes without any response from them, but when Fayed needed attention, they all came running. 'They were all there, nearby,' she says. 'They ignored my blood-curdling screams and went to help him as soon as he shouted in pain.'

No one should be in any doubt about whether Fayed's staff on that day knew what was going on. They knew what would happen and they stood back when it did. A teenager was sexually attacked while they stood by and did absolutely nothing. Even their basic humanity seemed to desert them, bought by the soiled dollars of a bully and a rapist.

No one, at any stage, asked Melissa how she was. She used the chaos that ensued after her bite to run for cover, heading for her room. 'I couldn't turn on the water or the lights. He'd ordered his staff to turn them off. Again, punishing me for defying him. His anger terrified me. He was so mad. I thought he might come in the night, and come and get me, maybe kill me.'

She heard her cabin door lock from the outside, so knew she was trapped. She spent the night wondering when he would come for her, and what he would do. At 4.30 a.m. someone knocked on her door, and she feared the worst. A key turned in the lock and a voice told her to get all her things together and leave the cabin. She emerged, cautiously, to find there was a boat to take her to land.

Just as she felt a wave of relief that she'd be getting on the boat and away from the yacht, she saw that in the boat that had arrived to take her to shore was another girl, around the same age as Melissa, pretty, with long, blonde hair. A replacement girl had been brought out. 'Another girl to the slaughterhouse. I realised that Fayed was trafficking women.'

While Melissa had been caught up in a nightmare on board the boat, back in London there was concern and confusion about her welfare. Her parents hadn't been contacted by Fayed despite his assurances that he'd spoken to them, so they had no idea where she was.

After her father called Fayed's office in Park Lane many times and was lied to by those to whom he spoke (they told him they had no idea where she was when they knew exactly), he went to see Thatcher, who asked to be kept informed. Then Melissa managed to get a message to her father that she was on her way home.

When she touched down at Heathrow, accompanied by Fayed's bodyguards, her father's security was there to meet her, alongside police officers.

The remarkable thing is that on the day she arrived back, the police knew what had happened and Fayed's security knew what had happened, but the story was buried. Melissa headed home and told her parents about everything. A decision was reached that it would be better for Melissa if no further action was taken. On the advice of her father she decided not to press charges, and she kept quiet.

Over the next few days all the gifts that Fayed had given her, plus many more that came the day after her return home, including a gift for her mother, were sent back, along with a letter from Melissa saying that she wouldn't be returning to her job, and that Fayed was not to contact her again. The letter was written by her father. He then drove her to Fayed's apartments, where the letter and the packages were left outside in full view of the cameras placed along the front of building, in the hope that he'd be embarrassed when security staff saw the footage.

Her father told Ronald and Nancy Reagan about the incident, and months later, at a lunch at Downing Street, Melissa spoke to the prime minister and told her what had happened. Thatcher already knew and expressed her disgust. 'I'd like to say that this was why he didn't get his British passport,' Melissa says. 'My parents knew how much he wanted one.'

Jack Straw, when home secretary, was one of those politicians to turn down Fayed's citizenship application. Fayed was twice denied British citizenship. He applied for a passport in 1995 and again in 1999 but failed to pass the 'good character' test required by the Home Office. There can be little question that his treatment of Melissa, as told to senior politicians and the Queen by the US ambassador, would have contributed to this, but it feels like a paltry recompense for what she went through.

Straw can't comment on whether the citizenship request was turned down because of the incident on Fayed's boat, but says it would have added to the number of serious complaints about him.

To get British citizenship there are various tests one must pass. First on the list is 'probity', the quality of possessing strong moral principles, honesty and decency. Fayed was judged to have a 'serious want of probity', according to Straw. This want of probity was demonstrated most succinctly in a damning Department of Trade and Industry (DTI) report into the takeover of Harrods. It concluded that Mr Fayed and his brother Ali had not been truthful about 'their origins, their wealth, their business interests and their resources'. Basically, they been deceitful about everything and their lives were built on a pack of lies.

What Melissa's story reveals is how confident Fayed was in his own invincibility. He had such a self-aggrandising view of the world that he knew he could take the daughter of one of America's most senior diplomats out of the country and abuse her, then bring her back, trembling at her experiences, and for nothing to happen to him. It's a dreadful fact that he was right. Nothing did happen to him. It may have contributed to him not getting British citizenship, but no one can say for definite. Certainly he wasn't arrested, no one spoke to him about what had happened and no one confronted him. As he predicted.

The story illuminates how easy it was for Fayed to feel invincible. He had security officers to protect him and knew that his money and new ranking in London society provided him with a shield.

The story also shows the extent to which other people knew what was happening. The person who booked

Melissa's trip and hotel room, and organised dinner in a quiet corner of the restaurant, the person who switched off the electricity in her room and the security guard who followed her down the hotel corridor . . . littered throughout the story are dozens of people who not only watched it all happen but assisted Fayed. They were accomplices to the crime.

Then there were the staff in the hotel and on the boat, the security guards close enough to hear a cry from Fayed and rush in to help, but who were not prepared to help when a teenage girl screamed. Why did they do that? How could any security officer justify such behaviour?

6

GUARDIAN OF SECRETS

THE SECURITY OFFICER

'They will never plant bombs at the store while
I am in charge. They are too scared of me.'

Fayed on the IRA

A man in a comfy navy-blue sweater is sitting in a large leather armchair next to the window in his Surrey home. 'Hello, I'm Biggie,' he says, rising to shake my hand with a struggle that hints at worn-out joints and aching limbs. He has a female friend with him, the person who let me in earlier.

He asks whether I mind if she stays during the interview. When I say that I'd rather she didn't, she jumps up like a hare startled by the crack of a twig and is out of the room in a flash. Biggie's eyes raise into his receding hairline and his mouth drops open. He looks so stunned by her sudden departure that he's momentarily lost for words.

As the sun streams through the window next to him, he screws his eyes up against the glare and pulls the blind down with more aggression than is needed. The whole scenario leaves me feeling like he deeply regrets his decision to meet me, and I can see why. I had several calls with him before our meeting in which I told him about the awful stories I had heard. I told him I needed to know why he and other security officers behaved like they did. Fayed wouldn't have been able to abuse women and get away with it if it hadn't been for men like Biggie. Why did they help him? Does he feel guilty?

Biggie was six foot four and around twenty stone when he worked as one of the 'generals' in Fayed's army of security officers. Today, he's still a powerfully built man with a strong jaw and deep-set dark eyes. He's now seventy, with craggy features and wisps of grey hair. He says he was into weight training and 'bulking up' when he was younger, which was very attractive to his employer. Fayed let him know several times that he liked how 'big, strong and brave' he was, 'like a warrior'.

Biggie was told that one day he'd be in charge of Fayed's security operation because of how fierce and loyal he was. He never did ascend to those dizzying heights, and he soon realised that such promises were made to everyone on Fayed's payroll. 'I think he said whatever he needed to say to get us to do what he wanted. The truth wasn't very important to him. Power and getting whatever he wanted were all that mattered.'

One of the tools that Fayed used to get what he wanted from the security team was cold, hard cash. Biggie says the pay was more than he'd have earned in similar roles elsewhere, so it was a good job financially, but what made it incredibly lucrative was that it was regularly topped up with 'bonus payments' – those famous brown envelopes that Fayed liked to hand out.

'We always used to joke that we couldn't fold our wallets because of the amount of notes we had in them,' he says. 'I've never been as well off as I was when working for Fayed. I'd bring home wodges of cash.'

But, the money, as with everything, was distributed with conditions attached. In return for fistfuls of £20 and £50 notes, absolute loyalty and secrecy were demanded, as was the need to do Fayed's bidding without questioning the boss's motivations.

'I was away all the time, working until late, spying on everyone, making sure he had whatever he wanted and whoever he wanted, wherever he was in the world. It was draining. I was never at home, and on the rare occasions I did make it through the door, I was stressed and angry with the world.'

The pictures on the mantlepiece next to us show Biggie as he was years ago: a photo of him in his twenties with his mates in the army, and a shot of him with an attractive wife and two lovely children next to him. His marriage split up while he was working for Harrods. He shrugs when I ask him about this.

'How anyone kept a relationship going while working for him is beyond me. And there was all this pressure on you to be single. He'd always say that wives were for producing children, and once you had children, you had no need for them. He also said that women would be provided for me if I needed them. The thing with the boss was that he wanted to be the most important person in everyone's lives, and I think he saw partners as an obstacle to that.'

Biggie went to work for Fayed in 1987, after a stint in the forces. He was recruited with three other soldiers with promises of money, prestige and the chance to travel to exotic locations.

'I'd been in Northern Ireland, standing in the freezing cold, terrified for my life. On the last tour a young child offered me a cup of tea. I took it gratefully, then realised it was full of powdered glass. I was newly married, and my wife hated my life in the army. Fayed's offer sounded great.' And when the Remembrance Day bombings happened in Enniskillen, badly injuring two of the men he'd served with, he felt confident that he'd done the right thing.

He soon became one of Fayed's leading men. 'The boss wanted information. He wanted to know where people were and what they were doing. Because I'd come straight from the army, I started off thinking he might be worried about IRA attacks.' When Biggie raised the subject, Fayed said, 'They will never plant bombs at the store while I am in charge. They are too scared of me.'

In 1983, two years before the Fayed brothers acquired the store, three police officers and three members of the public had been killed after an IRA car bomb attack outside a side entrance to Harrods. Then, in 1993, four people were injured when a bomb was placed in a litter bin outside the store. So, remarkably, the IRA weren't in the least bit scared of Fayed after all.

Biggie also thought Fayed must have installed all the surveillance equipment because he was paranoid about theft from the store, but he soon began to realise that this might not be the case when he noticed that all the people he was told to watch were 'young, blonde and very attractive'.

Biggie remembers being told to watch a woman called Julia, who worked in Fayed's personal office. He now realises it was because Fayed wanted to sleep with her. Julia* had been 'medically checked by the Harrods doctors', under the guise of being offered a free medical. Fayed had spoken to her and told her not to see her boyfriend or have sex with anyone else.

'It really hurt his massive ego when women who he fancied had boyfriends. He didn't like that at all. It was like he was saying, "I want you to be only with me . . . no one else." He was also madly anti-germs. If he'd had his way, he'd have had every woman in the building checked, cleaned, sterilised and bleached, then locked up until he was ready for them.

'With Julia he became quite obsessed about whether she was seeing anyone else, so he insisted that I send a guy out to follow her. The guy came back with a list of times, places and dates where Julia had been seen with her boyfriend. She was followed all over the place – in London and on a weekend away, to restaurants, etc. She didn't realise that everywhere she'd been, Fayed's man had been there too.'

As Biggie talks, there are a number of important questions hanging over us. Why didn't Biggie tell someone? Why didn't he speak out? Why didn't he go to the police? Or – simply – why didn't he refuse to behave in this way?

* Names followed by an asterisk indicate that the person's name has been changed to protect confidentiality.

'I didn't realise that Julia was going to be forced into sex with him. When he wanted us to check a woman out, he'd say, "She's someone I'd like to bring into my personal office, so I need to know what sort of person she is" – that was the information we had. We'd know he fancied the woman, but I didn't think we were lining up women to be raped. I never thought that. It's only now, many years later, that we realise what he was trying to get us to do.

'The other thing is – we knew that many of the women were being offered cash inducements, as we were, and given expensive handbags and jewellery. I thought it was all silly and flirty. I had no idea it was like this, and I'd swear to you that none of the others security guys did either.

'The guy who followed Julia was nicknamed "Sherlock", and he was the go-to person for investigations and stalking jobs. He was a decent guy. He wouldn't have got involved if he'd realised what he was doing.'

Biggie saw a lot during his time at the store, much of it sitting somewhat uncomfortably with his claim that he didn't know exactly what was going on. He says he witnessed girls coming out of Fayed's office crying, dishevelled and terrified. When I challenge him on this, he says, 'I should have known exactly what was happening, I accept that. Perhaps I turned a blind eye to it, but I was shocked when I watched the BBC documentary. I had no idea – no idea at all – that anything like that was happening.'

Even when people left his office crying?

'He was a stern boss. I thought maybe he'd told them off.'

Biggie says that Fayed was obsessed with sex, but in the way a schoolboy is – he loved anything phallic and was always 'teasing' male visitors to his office with a dildo he kept on his desk. But there was nothing warm or amusing about this. It was as if sex was a tool he used to embarrass and bully people.

As soon as Fayed saw a woman he was attracted to, Macnamara would tell security and her movements would be monitored and fed back to him. Then the woman would be moved up to work in Fayed's private office, and be lavished with gifts, money and attention until Fayed was ready to pounce.

According to Biggie, Fayed would refer to female staff he wanted to target for sex as 'non-typist secretaries', because although he moved them to his office, they weren't expected to do any typing. Many of the women I spoke to described moving into Fayed's office and not being at all sure what their job was. They sat there, doing a range of meaningless tasks, becoming increasingly unsure what was expected of them, while being watched and recorded at all times.

Tamara, who worked in the chairman's office in the 1990s, told the BBC that Fayed had the same way of working every day. He'd call one of the managers to find out which girls were working that day and then one of them would be called to his office. Another survivor has memories of the phone ringing in the office, and whoever was his main PA for the day would point at the chosen woman and send her up to Fayed's apartment.

The summons would be justified on the basis that Fayed wanted something to be brought up to him or that something had to be taken to the ground floor for him. He could have asked one of his ever-present security officers, like Biggie, to perform the chore, but he chose the prettiest girl in the office instead. Then, as Tamara says, 'You would be alone in that office, and it would be his opportunity to grope you, molest you.'

Away from the office, Biggie found himself working at many of Fayed's homes. There, he witnessed the comings and goings of women. He collected prostitutes from the station and returned them afterwards, he brought secretaries (typing and non-typing) to Fayed's house and he was told to watch the domestic staff – nannies, cooks and cleaners – to make sure he knew what they were doing at all times.

'There were recording devices everywhere: in his homes, his cars, in every office and every meeting room. They were in the flats he offered out to the prettiest girls to save them travelling home, and they were scattered throughout the store. There were people listening to them and reporting back. You had to be on your toes at all times. If Macnamara rang and asked where someone was or what was said in the meeting room the day before, you had to know. There was a huge pressure to know what people were doing.

'It got to the stage where not knowing where Sarah from Menswear had gone filled me with more terror than terrorist sightings in Northern Ireland.'

But it wasn't just voice recordings that Fayed wanted. There were the videos as well.

JANE

Jane worked at Harrods when she was seventeen and was invited to stay over in Fayed's apartment to save her from travelling home after a late night in the office. 'I had a problem with my back, so I was lying on my bed with my legs up against the wall and I was naked. The phone rang, and when I picked it up, Fayed was on the line. He said, "I like you lying like that." It just turned me cold.'

Jane talked to other women at the store who explained that there were cameras everywhere.

'The odd thing is that I knew that. It's one of the first things you get told when you start work, I just didn't think there would be cameras in the bedrooms of apartments being stayed in by female employees. It was all a shock.'

Jane decided she didn't want to work in Harrods's oppressive environment any more, and started to look for a new job. Then, one day, when coming into the store she was told to go straight to the office of one of Fayed's aides (who she has asked me not to name). There she found Macnamara waiting for her.

'He said, "We understand you're looking for another job. That's incredibly disloyal after everything the company has done for you. Nobody chooses to leave the chairman's employment; he chooses when you leave. So what we're going to do now is you're going to write a letter of resignation, and we're going to tell you what to write and you're going to write it, and you're going today. And that's it."

'It was the oddest thing. I was applying for jobs because I wanted to leave, and because of that, they wanted me to leave. So they stood over me, the two of them, and John [Macnamara] told me what to write.' She was then escorted off the shop floor by security guards and thrown onto the pavement 'like a criminal'.

'There was an incredible turnover of staff,' says Biggie. 'The boss would fall out with someone, not like the look of someone or need someone gone, and they would be straight out the door. He didn't seem to care about anyone.' Biggie's shoulders slump as he tells his stories. He's well aware of how awful they make him look. 'I'm just confirming everyone's worst fears about us, aren't I?'

Indeed.

He does, however, contest reports that Fayed's security guards were armed. He says they didn't carry guns, despite a number of accounts linking them to Walther PPK semi-automatic pistols, .38 inch revolvers and a range of Smith & Wesson handguns, as well as pump-action shotguns. There were even rumours of a shotgun disguised as a walking stick and machine guns obtained from the Middle East.

Fayed and firearms were even discussed in Parliament on 22 October 1998, after an article in the *Evening Standard* revealed that he'd established links with a gun club in order to justify and legalise his ownership of guns.

'This House,' read the Early Day Motion, '. . . is disturbed that Mr Fayed established the bogus Park Lane

Gun Club to legalise the possession by his employees of semi-automatic pistols with extended magazines.'

But Biggie insists that he never saw guns during his time with Fayed. Even when I suggest that there may have been guns that he didn't see, he says that isn't the case. 'I was fairly senior. I'd have known if there were guns. Also, I was ex-military, so I'd have been one of the guys carrying if there had been guns floating around.'

Dr Jerry Hart is global head of security for a Swiss multinational corporation. He's dubious about the notion that Fayed's security team carried guns. 'No, I don't believe they would have been armed. Overseas, yes, but not in this country. When it comes to firearms – or any weapon – the same rules apply to corporate and close-protection officers as to any other person. You'd go to prison if you were caught. Anyone who has armed officers in their employ-ment would themselves also be responsible. To be honest, you'd have a police SWAT team descending on you because you posed an armed threat. There would be mass arrests. No security professional would put themselves at this risk, only professional criminals.'

Hart refers to the fact that Prince Harry wanted to use bodyguards on his trips to the UK. Private security officers can't carry guns, so Harry wanted the government to loosen policy and allow his guys to carry while protecting him, but he was told it wasn't possible.

'If they felt so strongly about security officers not carry-ing guns to protect a member of the royal family, I'm damn sure they wouldn't have turned a blind eye to Fayed having an army of armed officers,' says Dr Hart. 'If a foreign president comes to visit, accompanied by military police armed guards, they have to hand guns over at the airport. The same with private security personnel.'

He also points out the difference between private and corporate security. 'Private security tends to be rent-out security – like G4. You hire them to protect a service or an individual. They act in self-defence to ensure the person they are protecting stays safe. Their main issue is to keep the person away from trouble. Corporate security is different. That's dealing with internal threats – robbery, fraud, burglary, blackmail, kidnapping, as well as insider dealing and disclosing information to competitors. A lot of companies have a corporate security set-up to keep control.

'The police can't enter your home unless you invite them in, or they have reasonable grounds to believe that a crime is taking place. This is the same with corporate environments – you have to be invited in and you can't fish for crime. So it's the corporate team who will conduct the internal investigation because they're free to roam through the business in a way the police are not. It means the company can find out exactly what's going on before handing it over to law enforcement.'

Biggie deeply regrets the role he played in Fayed's abusive rein at Harrods, though it feels rather late in the day for such apologies. He says that by speaking out, he hopes that there will be a realisation of how bad Fayed was and how reckless he was with the lives of young women.

'I don't feel proud saying this, but the truth is that no one cared about the women because Fayed didn't care, and we were taught to do everything Fayed wanted. He didn't have an elite group of highly trained security officers – the staff was made up mainly of ex-coppers and soldiers, who had been trained to do everything asked of them without question. I was young and he was in charge, and we'd come from a system where the more experienced guys said, "Jump" and you'd ask, "How high?" The boss used to call the women "prostitutes", and I suppose I genuinely thought that a lot of them were.

'Perhaps I should have been more questioning. Well, no, I definitely should have been, now that we know what was going on. But I was young, being paid well, and doing what I was told.'

Biggie's testimony helps to explain the power that Fayed had by recruiting a security team predominantly made up of men who were used to obeying orders without question. He brought them in from the army and the police and gave precise instructions that they followed.

Fayed oiled the wheels with the regular supply of bungs in little brown envelopes, and the prospect of more money, promotions and better foreign trips were held aloft before them to encourage them further.

The largely unquestioning nature of the security team was a great asset to him. The other great asset was the way in which he was able to use this security team to influence the police, keep them on side and keep himself out of trouble.

7

BADGES AND BRIBES

POLICE COMPLICITY

'Macnamara was a thoroughly nasty, evil man who
would do anything for Fayed. He wouldn't have
been out of place in the Stasi.'

Biggie, a former Harrods security guard, on
former police officer John Macnamara

In the corridors of New Scotland Yard, the Metropolitan Police is being forced to confront its past. The public outcry following *Al Fayed: Predator at Harrods*, the BBC documentary that contained serious allegations about Fayed and the complicity of former police officers, has reached crisis point.

The battle the force now faces is threefold: first, to establish exactly what happened when so many women came in to police stations to report crimes decades ago, and whether they were dealt with properly. Second, it has the task of looking at the hundreds of new complaints that have come in since Fayed's death. Finally, the police need to establish who helped Fayed. Who on Fayed's staff, in the words of Commander Stephen Clayman of the Met, 'facilitated or enabled' criminal acts, and what should happen to them? Surely criminal charges will be brought. But while establishing who at Harrods 'facilitated or enabled' criminal acts, the police need also to look inwards, towards themselves and their own culpability. If the police had acted in a responsible, professional way and not allowed Fayed to slip through gaps time and again, would he have been able to carry on behaving as he did?

There's no way to sugarcoat it. The close links between certain serving and past Metropolitan Police officers and key members of Fayed's security team allowed Fayed to carry out his criminal behaviour uninhibited by the law. Indeed, the raft of relationships between the Harrods security team and police officers is one of the central elements in understanding how Fayed got away with his criminal activity for so long.

This is not to suggest that all officers and security personnel connected to Harrods and Fayed were culpable, but there were sufficient individuals within both groups to create a complicated web that prevented the lies and dishonesty from getting out, ensuring that Fayed would never be caught and punished.

And the whole rotten structure was constructed by John Macnamara.

'Macnamara was a thoroughly nasty, evil man who would do anything for Fayed,' says Biggie. 'He wouldn't have been out of place in the Stasi. I remember him threatening women that if they spoke out, he would find out about it and they'd live to regret it. If they did go to the police, he'd know immediately because of his network of contacts. One time a woman went to the police, and Mac got a call to say she was there, and he was outside the nick before she'd even been released. He had a chat to her and she went back in and dropped the charges against Fayed.'

Macnamara was often at Chelsea and West End Central police stations, where he exerted considerable control.

John* worked at Chelsea Police Station in the early 1990s and became familiar with the sight and sound of Macnamara. 'He came to police meet-ups in the pub and bought drinks – he knew the station commander well and looked after everyone. I was junior at the time and didn't have much to do with him, but I had just done PNC training [the training required to access information on the Police National Computer] so would have to handle the requests to access the PNC from senior officers.'

Even though all officers were told unequivocally that the police computer could only be used for police business, and that misuse would result in dismissal, John received frequent requests for information that had nothing to do with crime. He came to realise these were for Macnamara.

'The requests would come from my boss, who would instruct me to provide data,' says John. 'I knew when they had come through Macnamara because there were no details. You'd usually have the background context on why the research needed to be conducted, but when they were for him there would be no background material – just the name and a request to search for findings.

'I didn't do that many of them, I guess most of them were done by more senior officers, but when I did do them I worried about the audit trail.

'I'd heard all the stories about officers getting in trouble. One guy went onto the system to check his ex's new boyfriend, and when they found out, he was sacked. Nothing ever happened to me, though.'

Hannah Wright, a police spokesperson, said: 'That wouldn't happen today. Now everybody has a unique ID to log on to the National Computer, and we can monitor who accesses every single card . . . if they haven't got a policing purpose, questions will be asked.'

No one asked any questions when John was accessing the computer for Macnamara, however, because everyone was beholden to the former detective chief superintendent. 'No one said no to Macnamara,' recalls John, 'because they'd worked with him as their superior and I guess they still thought of him as being senior. Also, they liked him because he looked after everyone. He sent hampers to the station, he gave bundles of notes to officers who helped him. There would be cash in brown envelopes. I wasn't paid or anything – I was bottom rung of the ladder – but I was handed a card with £100 in it at Christmas, and a bottle of Scotch or something like that. It was probably very expensive, but I didn't drink Scotch so I gave it to my dad. It was from Harrods.'

There are varying accounts of how much the police were paid for their work. Biggie recalls officers being paid a great deal, but John thinks it was more like £100 every time they offered assistance. 'That money came on top of Harrods food hampers arriving at the police station – some of those were worth a lot of money. I've heard some of them were worth around £800. In addition to that, gifts from the store were offered – free suits, handbags, perfumes and cosmetics. Then there were trips to the Ritz in Paris for senior officers.'

Those who were particularly helpful would be offered jobs at Harrods. It was a great system, and it worked beautifully . . . for the police and the security team. Not so much for the many hundreds of people who were abused, degraded and bullied by Fayed, and certainly not for those who were kidnapped and raped. When the police collude with criminals, the world becomes a very dark place.

Nowhere was this clearer than in the police's handling of complaints against Fayed. The Met say they received complaints about Fayed between 2005 and 2023. There were twenty-one separate allegations of abuse: four of rape, sixteen of sexual assaults and one related to human trafficking.

Officers went to the Crown Prosecution Service (CPS) in search of advice in relation to ten of these allegations, and the CPS judged that there was enough evidence for only two of the files to be passed on to them. No charges were brought. As for the other allegations, no further action was taken.

Fayed was investigated by the police three times yet was never prosecuted. In 2008 he was accused of sexually assaulting a fifteen-year-old girl in the Harrods board-room. The CPS said there wasn't enough evidence to prosecute, citing 'conflicting evidence'. In 2015 the Metropolitan Police investigated him following allegations he'd raped a woman in 2013. Once again, the CPS reviewed the files and there was no prosecution. In 2018 multiple women came forward to tell their stories to the police. That time, a file didn't even get as far as the CPS.

While the CPS did review their Fayed files, a spokesperson said, 'To bring a prosecution, the CPS must be confident there is a realistic prospect of conviction – in each instance, our prosecutors looked carefully at the evidence and concluded this wasn't the case.'

SAMANTHA-JANE

Senior Metropolitan police officers claimed that the first allegation against Fayed was in 2005, but it has emerged that the first complaints were made over a decade earlier. In 1995 Samantha-Jane Ramsay went to the police about Fayed's behaviour, but police have no record of her report. Her story is heart-breaking.

Samantha-Jane was seventeen when she moved to London to work in the toy department at Harrods. It was a dream job, but soon after starting at the store, Fayed spotted her and invited her to his office. While she was there, he offered her a bundle of bank notes and told her she could come and work directly for him. Would she like that? He told her to think about it. Then he invited her to come back in for a second meeting to discuss his proposal. This time, he told her she needed to have a medical examination and advised her to wash with Dettol. Having dispensed these words of wisdom, he sexually assaulted her.

Samantha-Jane rushed out of the room and told her supervisor, who said, 'Not another one.' She was then taken to a room where Fayed, who'd been told of her talk with her supervisor, was waiting, furious with her. He fired her on the spot, adding, 'You will not tell anyone about this – we know where you live.'

Samantha-Jane reported the assault to officers at Marylebone Police Station the following day. They took her details but dismissed her case. She was told that Fayed was too powerful, and if it came down to her word against his, he would win. One officer told her that there had been a lot of complaints before and they had 'files inches high' on Fayed.

So, not only was Samantha-Jane's attack ten years earlier than the ones the police remember, but she was clearly not the first complainant. If there were files that were 'inches high' in 1995, we can assume that plenty of complaints had been made in the late 80s and early 90s. Samantha-Jane heard nothing more from the Met Police so, on the advice of a retired police officer, talked to police in Gosport, close to her family home. They passed on her report to the Met but nothing ever happened. In frustration, Samantha-Jane spoke to the *News of the World* in 1998, hoping that publicising her case would persuade the police to take action. Her decision to talk to journalists at the Sunday paper means there is now a public record of the account, but it didn't prompt any action from the police.

The whole incident deeply affected Samantha-Jane, who became quiet and withdrawn, exhibited erratic behaviour and jumped between jobs, unable to settle. She was unstable and restless, and even tried to commit suicide. She was a broken woman.

Samantha-Jane died in a car crash in 2007 when she was just twenty-eight years old. Her family feel that, though the death was registered as an accident, Samantha-Jane took her own life. Her mother Wendy told the BBC, 'Her spark had gone. The ray of light that she always had was dimming. The more time that passed from the incident, the dimmer it got.' According to Samantha-Jane's sister Emma, 'It really changed her outlook on life, and we had twelve years of erratic behaviour after that, a suicide attempt, and never really finding her place. She was never right after what happened in London.'

Why was action not taken by the Met Police? Why were there no dismissals of police officers, no concerted effort to smash the cosy club that existed between Harrods and the police? Many women were abused, drugged and raped after the information about Samantha-Jane's assault was reported. That could all have been stopped. The Met say they are unable to comment, and that everything is being investigated. But it's not as if the relationship between the police and Harrods was any great secret that now needs to be decoded. By the mid-1990s it had all been documented in the 'Loftus report', also known as the '*Vanity Fair* report'.

This in-depth document is crucial to understanding everything that was going on between serving police officers and security officers at Harrods at the time. The author of the report was a man called Bob Loftus, a former major in the Royal Military Police who'd worked for Fayed since 1987. He held a senior position, as security director, then in February 1996 he was dismissed. Fayed accused him of a range of offences, including taking drugs, sexual abuse and even breaking into Tiny Rowland's safe deposit box at Harrods in 1995.

Loftus took legal action, and Fayed was forced to accept that the allegations were totally unfounded and agreed to pay damages and legal costs. So the relationship between Loftus and Fayed was, to put it mildly, strained. Loftus's dismissal from Harrods coincided with Fayed's attempts to sue *Vanity Fair* after their portrayal of him twelve months earlier. The magazine was putting together as much evidence as possible to defend their article. It didn't take *Vanity Fair* and its lawyer David Hooper long to realise how much Loftus knew, and approach him.

Fayed was appalled at the idea of Loftus helping *Vanity Fair*, so to prevent Loftus speaking out Fayed offered him £90,000 to keep quiet. But Loftus refused and spoke to Hooper, revealing the extent of the racism and sexual harassment that had taken place while he worked at the store, and confirming that a huge amount of spying on staff and recording them had occurred. To prove how bad it was, he produced 320 tapes that contained hundreds of conversations Fayed had covertly recorded.

Finally, he outlined the importance of the relationships between Harrods and the police. His witness statement was over fifty pages long, and ran through what was happening at the store and how the police were often involved in assisting Fayed. The report was shocking at the time, and remains shocking today.

Loftus's allegations about Fayed's control of the police fall into three key categories:

Bribery and corruption: Loftus outlined the inappropriate relationships Fayed and his staff developed with certain serving Metropolitan Police officers. He confirmed that cash and gifts were routinely given to officers in return for favourable services for Harrods, including access to the Police National Computer and the provision of sensitive information. According to Loftus, detectives received mobile phones from Harrods that were bugged to record conversations. These recordings, which allegedly contain definitive proof of police involvement, were among those submitted by Loftus to verify his claims.

Wrongful arrests: Loftus alleged that Fayed's security team collaborated with compromised police officers to falsely accuse and arrest employees.

Intervention by senior police officers: Former Metropolitan Police Commissioner Sir David McNee intervened in legal matters to protect Fayed's interests.

One example of police intervention was cited in the report. In June 1993 Salah, Fayed's brother, left a shoulder bag in a taxi while travelling north from Aberdeen Airport to Fayed's castle. The driver, a special constable, handed the bag in at the nearest police station. Inside they discovered crack cocaine, a homemade pipe and white tablets.

A deal was struck with the police that they would say the bag was owned by Rachel Crowe, a Harrods executive trainee. She was charged with possession of the items, despite clear indications that she had no knowledge of the drugs and paraphernalia. A few weeks later Loftus was informed by the investigating detective that no further action would be taken against Crowe. He said that Commissioner McNee used his influence to ensure the case was dropped. To add to the ugliness of the whole incident, it became clear afterwards that Crowe had been physically assaulted by Salah but had been paid to remain silent.

Some of the most difficult stories to listen to are those about young victims who turned to the police for advice. When a child under the age of eighteen goes to a police station to report a serious crime, the child protection services should be notified and interviews should be conducted by those with expertise in talking to young people. The interviews should not be carried out in police stations but in separate buildings specifically designed to help young people overcome their fears and speak out.

This is the case now, and it has been the case since the early 1990s, following the implementation of the Children Act 1989. In 1992 the 'Memorandum of Good Practice on Video Recorded Interviews with Child Witnesses for Criminal Proceedings' was introduced, which established guidelines for joint interviews between social workers and police. This helped move interviews away from police stations to more child-friendly environments.

But none of the young people sharing their experiences recall being introduced to child protection officers. Some of them were shocked to leave the police station after not being taken seriously by the officers within, only to find Harrods security personnel waiting in the car park, having been tipped off by the police. Many of the women said that after reporting the crime they never heard anything from the police again.

Police spokesperson Hannah Wright comments that things shouldn't have happened like that: 'If you report a crime, you should be given a CAD [computer aided dispatch] number so that anybody looking back, including an officer or member of public, can see what was reported and when.' That simply didn't happen when the women reported Fayed to the police.

The Metropolitan Police say they cannot comment on the Loftus report because, despite it having been written over a decade ago, they only received it just before Christmas 2024.

PELHAM

One of the women who went to the police and has spoken out about what happened is Pelham Spong, an American who alleged that Fayed assaulted her after she was recruited for a position at Harrods. She travelled to

London from Paris in 2008 for the job and was immediately told that as part of the process she must undergo a gynaecological examination, to be conducted by Dr Wendy Snell. The examination identified an infection, for which she was prescribed antibiotics.

Following the examination, she was summoned to Fayed's office, where he told her he saw great potential in her and offered to fund her education and career advancement in exchange for a sexual relationship. Wearing a silk dressing gown, he asked whether she had 'taken care' of the infection. When she attempted to deflect his advances, he grabbed her face and forcibly kissed her.

Spong told the BBC she approached the police in 2017, but officers claimed they were 'unable to obtain an account from the suspect due to his poor state of health'. Fayed's assistant also refused to provide a statement. Detective Inspector Debbie McCormack stated that the case would not be referred to the Crown Prosecution Service as there was no 'realistic chance of conviction'.

This infuriated Spong, who had provided a file to the police containing emails, letters and medical records, which included names of employees and doctors. She later filed a complaint with the Independent Office for Police Conduct (IOPC), alleging investigative failures. These included the police's failure to obtain formal statements from key witnesses and the fact they sought employment records from the wrong company. She also filed a complaint with the General Medical Council (GMC), which responded that it had no jurisdiction over whether a gynaecological examination should have been part of the hiring process, but acknowledged her distress that Fayed had been informed of her medical history.

One of the most alarming facets of the relationship between Fayed and the police is how blatant it was; neither he nor the police appear to have done anything to hide how closely they were working together. Fayed even gave the police new panda cars, with 'This car is sponsored by Harrods' emblazoned on the side. Superintendent Peter Dowse received the keys from Fayed and told waiting journalists that sponsorship did not compromise police ethics. 'We look very carefully at who we would accept sponsorship from,' he said, 'and we are only too delighted to accept it from Harrods.'

According to Stephen Otter, a chief superintendent with the force at the time, 'It looked more like a Harrods vehicle than a police vehicle. It looked like someone had put a blue light on a Harrods vehicle.' He thought the whole arrangement was ridiculous, so he headed over to Harrods to hand back the vehicle, but he was told by the security officer there that the car was part of an arrangement that had been going on for a long time. He said he was told, 'When you've been here a bit longer, you will have a better understanding of this relationship.'

Otter also commented on the 'jail' in the basement of Harrods, saying it 'was better than any detention centre I'd seen in the whole Metropolitan Police. I just felt deeply uncomfortable with the relationship. It was a relationship in which this department store had huge amounts of power over the leaders of the areas of policing around them. It felt like a corrupt relationship on both sides.'

In response to criticism about its handling of the complaints against Fayed, a police spokesperson said: 'The Metropolitan Police is committed to thoroughly reviewing all information relating to historical allegations in the case of Mohamed Al Fayed, which includes our Directorate of Professional Standards assessing any indication of police misconduct. In line with this, we always look to acquire relevant documents, including witness statements, and other materials which we will actively review.'

8

CLINICAL VIOLATIONS

THE DOCTORS AND THEIR PURITY TESTS

'And – do you have a boyfriend?
Do you have sex with him?'

Fayed to Jayne

Only in the most uncivilised of societies are there doctors who cannot be trusted. Freedom from doubt is a prerequisite for the functioning of a healthy patient–doctor relationship. Patients throw their health, their very lives, into a doctor's care, and they trust in turn that the doctor will do their utmost to safeguard and preserve it.

And so, neatly, to Harrods, that most uncivilised of societies. Here, with their Hippocratic oaths still warm on their breath, the store's doctors would conduct intimate tests on the bodies of hundreds of women, all for the chairman's pleasure. It's hard to imagine, hard to absorb the seriousness of the betrayal of the doctors employed by Fayed.

But the truth is that when many women started work at Harrods, they were required to endure a medical that included an intimate examination at the chairman's request. The results of the internal tests, which examined for HIV and all sexually transmitted diseases, were subsequently passed to Fayed. Many women never received these results; they weren't for them. They were for the chairman.

SARAH

Sarah began a job in marketing for Harrods in 1994.

'On my first day at Harrods I was told that I had to have a medical. It seemed strange, there's no doubt about that. I was joining in order to do an office-based job. I didn't know why a medical examination was necessary, but it was made very clear to me that if I didn't have a medical, I couldn't do the job.

'I remembering saying, "Are you serious? Are you really telling me that I won't be able to take up this job that I've signed a contract for if I don't have a medical that no one told me I needed to have?"

'The answer was, "Yes. It's vital." The reasons were baffling. The chairman's son was very sensitive to germs, and Fayed wanted to make sure that everyone in the work-force was fit and healthy and had the opportunity for a full medical check-up.

'I went to have the medical and I remember doing a urine test, which is a bit bizarre if you think about it, did bloods, and then I remember Wendy Snell saying to me, "Are you up to date with your smear test?" To be honest with you, I couldn't remember, so she said, "I'll tell you what, we can do all of that for you. Why don't I just do a complete check for you down there?"

'I always thought it was the weirdest thing, but I put it out of my mind and got on with the job. Then, when I watched the BBC's documentary about Harrods, I saw all the girls talking about the smear tests. What happened to me all those years ago suddenly felt like abuse. They were calling them "purity tests". The doctors were testing us to make sure we were fit for rape. I felt violated. How could the doctors do that? How could they?'

Presumably for the same reason as everyone else in this sordid tale. Because of fear, or for money.

JAYNE

Jayne* began working at Harrods as a clerical assistant in 1996, a day after her sixteenth birthday. On the day she started, she was called into Fayed's office and asked how she was getting on. She'd only been in the store for half a day so she says she smiled and told him that everything was fine.

'Good,' he said. 'If anything is not fine, you must come to me. Only me. I will sort out any problems.'

She was delighted to hear this. 'I didn't expect the chairman to be so directly involved in my employment. I thought it was really nice that he cared.' Then things changed.

'And – do you have a boyfriend?' Fayed asked. 'Do you have sex with him?' Jayne was a virgin and had no desire to discuss that with Fayed. 'I think I just looked at him blankly. I don't think I said anything, then he told me I could go.'

A few hours later one of Fayed's PAs contacted her and told her she would need to go for a company medical. It would take place in Harley Street. 'It's a perk of working for Harrods,' she was told.

'OK, when is my appointment?'

'Now,' she was told.

A basic medical was done, then she was told an internal examination would be needed to test for sexually transmitted infections, including HIV. Jayne explained that she was a virgin, but the doctor insisted it was necessary, so the intrusive examination took place.

'I bled a lot,' said Jayne. 'I found it really painful, and all the doctor said was, "Oh, so you *are* a virgin."'

Jayne went straight back to the office and was called in by Fayed before she'd even had time to take her coat off. 'He wanted to talk to me about the examination I'd had. He knew that I'd bled during it.'

Discussing the intimate details of her medical exam and being questioned on her 'purity' was highly embarrassing. She found the conversation confusing, intrusive and humiliating. 'I couldn't think how he'd know, other than that the doctor phoned him as soon as I left and updated him. It was horrible. I felt like crying, but I did think that would be the end of it.'

Two weeks later Jayne received a call from one of Fayed's PAs telling her to go to his Park Lane apartment. When she first walked in, Fayed seemed very civilised, but then he became aggressive. 'He said he'd like to have sex with me. I said no, and he instantly became angry. His whole face changed. He was, like, really furious. I guess he didn't like anyone saying no to him. He was holding me tightly and I told him he was hurting me, but that made him squeeze me even more.'

Jayne tried to pull away, which angered him further. He put one hand on her chest, pushed her back against the sofa cushions and raped her. 'I was trying so hard to get away. I don't think I was very strong when I was sixteen, and I was terrified, utterly terrified, which made me weaker. I kept struggling all the time, but nothing made him stop.'

Jayne knows that there were security officers outside the locked door. She's also sure that the PA who sent her up to Fayed's apartment knew what would happen.

'But it's the doctor who I feel most angry about. She did a test I didn't need, which caused me great pain, then passed the private information to Fayed, giving him the all-clear he needed. When it comes to the rape – that's all his fault – and I hope he's rotting in hell, but there are other people who were part of the crime. The doctor checked that I was OK to be raped, and told him I was. Whichever way you choose to look at this, that's what happened.'

*　　*　　*

When Fayed bought Harrods in 1985, the woman running the occupational health department was Dr Jenny Duckham. Duckham says that the department ran like any other medical set-up within a business, offering a service to members of staff who needed it. They tended to cuts and headaches, did eye tests and cardiac checks.

Then Fayed took over, and everything changed. Soon after his arrival, a member of the HR department asked her whether she would carry out gynaecological tests on women. Duckham refused, asking why on earth that needed to be done. She was told, 'Don't worry about it, we'll deal with it' by the HR official, who quickly scuttled away, knowing the question was inappropriate.

She assumed that was the end of it, and put it down to him being 'a dirty old man'. But he simply outsourced the tests to Harley Street doctors willing to do them, and in 1991 he sacked Duckham and closed down the occupational health department.

'Harrods had the oldest occupational health department of any retail store in London, it had a wonderful history of caring for the staff,' Duckham told *The Times*. 'When people grew too old for work, arrangements were made to put them in nice old people's homes. It was a really nice environment. And then he took over and things began to wobble. The atmosphere changed and became anxious. But of course I had no idea of the extent of what was going on.'

After closing the occupation health department, Fayed kept on one nurse, working from the infamous basement of the store.

During the month that Duckham was obliged to work at Harrods following her sacking she was at pains to hide confidential medical information from Fayed, so she shredded it all, taking piles of papers home with her to rip up in the privacy of her own home.

'I was worried that they would be misused,' she said.

SANDRA

Sandra had her internal examination when she started work at the store, and was told by Dr Wendy Snell that she had an STI (sexually transmitted infection) and that she shouldn't sleep with her boyfriend. Sarah firmly believes that Snell made this up so that she would refrain from sexual activity and thus be 'clean' for Fayed.

Soon afterwards she was invited to accompany Fayed to the Ritz in Paris as his PA. He raped her while she was there. He told her that she was lucky he was willing to sleep with her, considering she had an STI. Sandra was devastated by the rape, but there was something else that was bothering her – she knew that Fayed was fastidious about cleanliness and would never have slept with her had he known she had a disease.

'I suddenly thought to myself, "It wasn't true. It wasn't true that I had an STI. It can't have been."' It also struck her that the doctor at no time gave her any medicine or referred her to a gynaecologist for further treatment.

Sandra had been with her boyfriend for five years, so when she'd heard about the STI, she accused her boyfriend of cheating. 'We ended up splitting up because of it. Then I called him and asked him to go to his own doctor, and I went to mine. Neither of us had an STI. It had all been made up.'

EMMA

In 2008 Emma* was given a medical by Harrods before starting a new job. As part of the medical she was swabbed for STIs and asked to give blood and urine samples. The swab showed that she had an infection.

'I was concerned,' she recalls, 'so I double-checked with the doctor that this information wouldn't be shared with anyone. The doctor assured me that it was confidential.'

Soon after that, Emma was called to see the chairman in his apartment. She arrived to find him decked out in a blue dressing gown. He told her to take a seat, and held her hand.

'Did you get yourself sorted out?' he asked.

Emma had no idea what he was talking about.

'You know – the problem down there,' he said, pointing at Emma's groin. 'Is it taken care of? Did you take the medicine?'

Emma described herself as being 'open-mouthed' and says that there was no way he could possibly have known about her infection unless the doctor had told him.

'I can sleep with you now,' he said, 'if you have taken the medicine.'

She rushed out of his office and resigned from her job. She tried to bury the memory but remained horrified by what had happened.

Nine years later, after Fayed had sold Harrods, she heard stories emerging about other women who'd endured the same internal examination, so she decided she would contact the GMC and register a complaint.

'I wanted to add my voice to those who were speaking out, and it had upset me a lot. I'd lost a lot of trust in people since those days and certainly didn't trust doctors in the same way I had, so I thought it best to do something.'

She contacted the GMC but feels she was 'fobbed off'. They told her:

We cannot normally investigate concerns about incidents that happened more than five years ago, unless it is in the greater public interest to do so. In this case, the concerns you have raised about the doctors would not fulfil the criteria for us to waive that rule. We recognise that you are distressed that Mr Al Fayed knew about your medical history. However, we have no powers to investigate or resolve whether he was given that information by the doctors or if he obtained it by other means, especially after this passage of time.

But that wasn't the only complaint levelled at the GMC. Another woman said she sent in a complaint and received a similar response, and she has been told that there were two other complaints lodged. Enough, surely, for the GMC to 'waive that rule'.

There were a number of doctors working at Harrods. Snell was the doctor who performed the examination on Sarah, but she wasn't alone; four female doctors and two male doctors did the tests.

Dr Snell has since died but the other doctor who worked at Harrods remains registered with the General Medical Council, and several women say they intend to make a formal complaint about her. She has refused requests for comment from all areas of the media. I have called her several times by phone and delivered a note to her door, but she has not responded.

The GMC said the allegations were 'deeply concerning'. It seems an inadequate response given the severity of the accusations against one of their number. They later updated this to give a more substantial comment:

> The alleged sexual abuse conducted by Mohamed Al Fayed against multiple women is horrifying. The allegations relating to medical staff working for Mr Al Fayed are deeply concerning. If we identify any potential fitness to practise concerns about individual doctors, we will thoroughly examine all relevant information and take action as appropriate.

Fayed's use of doctors to 'check out' potential rape targets was a grotesque infringement of the rights of his staff. He did it, ostensibly, because of his fastidious nature and obsessiveness about cleanliness, but the way in which he used the information – telling women that he knew the results before them, giving them the medicine they required, and enquiring into the results – all hint at another use of the medical information – to further control and dominate his employees.

By having the results of private medical tests before them, and revealing their results to them, he was able to demonstrate that he knew everything, he was in control, they were just pawns in his game.

9

EMPIRE OF FEAR

HARRODS IN THE 80s

'I don't want any apes or gorillas on the floor, and no Pakis. The cripples and fatties can go. The girls must be slim, white, good-looking, and they must talk properly. I will be watching to make sure.'

Fayed to Joanna, when she and her friend Rachel went to work for him at Harrods in 1988

The security operation was firmly in place, the doctors and members of the police force were working in his favour, so now it was time for Fayed to set about organising his staff. Fayed had a very clear vision of the sort of people he wanted to have working at Harrods, and he was unafraid to express this in the strongest, most offensive terms.

'I don't want any apes or gorillas on the floor, and no Pakis. The cripples and fatties can go,' he told Joanna, when she and her friend Rachel went to work for him in 1988. 'The girls must be slim, white, good-looking and they must talk properly. I will be watching to make sure.'

RACHEL AND JOANNA

Rachel is in tears even before she utters a word. She wipes at her eyes and apologises. 'Do I look a complete state?' She doesn't. She's one of these beautiful people who looks good even when crying.

Rachel was offered a job on the ground floor of Harrods – the notorious beauty floor – in 1988 and was told that, if she worked hard, and did everything that was asked of her, she would be promoted and offered a job in the buying department. Six months later she left, having been sexually abused by Fayed and a Qatari friend of his, then marched out of the store when she refused to cooperate further.

'I was put into the "jail" in the basement, then sacked for shoplifting. I've never shoplifted in my life and I didn't then. They placed items into my handbag and accused me of stealing them. I lived with deep shame after that. I was terrified to apply for jobs in case they asked for a reference from Harrods and my "crime" was revealed.'

It's extraordinary that Fayed would stoop so low and cause such anguish in order to get rid of someone he'd abused, but this wasn't an isolated incident.

'A lot of the women were sacked after he attacked them, accused of things they didn't do. That's something we have come up against time and again,' said Richard Meeran, of the Leigh Day law firm, who is representing many of the women raped by Fayed.

'It deeply affected my life,' says Rachel. 'And for what? So some filthy old Egyptian could live out his teenage fantasies? I loathe him more than I ever imagined being able to loathe anyone.'

Joanna is next to Rachel and agrees that 'loathsome' is a good word to describe their former boss. Joanna is small, with shiny conker-coloured hair fashioned into a neat bob.

She pulls at the cuffs of her jumper, pulling them down until they cover her hands.

'I have survivor's guilt about the whole thing,' she says. 'I feel like I knew what was going on. I'd heard the stories but didn't say anything. They were all rumours so I didn't feel as if I could speak out, but I should have said something.'

But to whom? Who would listen to a young woman complaining about her boss because of rumours she'd heard?

'I was never abused by Fayed. I wasn't his type. I was too small, too round and too dark.' She smiles at Rachel, whose long, slim legs are crossed at the ankle. She has blonde hair, tied at the nape of her neck. The way she peeps out from under her fringe is immediately reminiscent of Princess Diana. 'The knock-out beauties like Rache were the ones in danger,' she adds.

Joanna says she knew that something was wrong at Harrods from the start, and this was compounded when she was told by a senior employee, 'Watch out for these girls. They are in danger.'

The words were whispered in a clandestine way, but Joanna knew what the lady meant. 'I relive the moment all the time . . . that's the point at which I should have said, "What do you mean, 'They are in danger'? We need to go to the police." But I didn't do that.'

'You can't blame yourself,' Rachel reassures her. 'You were a kid like the rest of us. He was terrifying. If you'd done anything, you'd have got into the most enormous trouble, and I doubt it would have helped us in any way.'

'Yes, I guess,' says Joanna, 'but the amount of hatred in that place was insane.'

Joanna was moved from the shop floor to help with recruitment for the Christmas rush, and was given clear directions from a senior HR official at the time. 'No niggers, no Pakis, no gays, no ugly people and no fatties. If you bring these people on board, you'll lose your job.'

'I was startled when she said it, but – again – I didn't say anything. Instead, I selected all the right people for the store, hunting out white, slender, attractive women, preferably blondes.

'I was told the reason for this was that the sales staff needed to reflect the customers in the store, and since most customers were tall, blonde and elegant, the staff needed to be too. I don't think that was true at all, but it didn't occur to me to question it at the time – I recruited the sales staff they wanted. Now I realise I was his pimp, effectively.'

Joanna says that lots was going on behind the scenes that people didn't know about. 'People were being checked out and checked up on all the time. I was promoted and sent on store walks. My job was to identify women who would be good for the chairman's office. Once we'd identified someone, they would be invited up, given cash bonuses and a made-up job, all their calls were taped and they were watched wherever they went. I mean – they were watched everywhere. They couldn't go to the loo without the boss knowing. Everything was on camera.

'Then, one by one, they would be called to the chairman's office where he propositioned them. I think some of the staff knew what was happening – they had to know. But it was such an achievement to be working at Harrods that none of us wanted to leave. I did leave, eventually, and as I got older and worked for other companies, I realised how vile Harrods was.

'When you're younger you don't know any different. You know it feels cruel and horrible, but you don't know whether this is how work is. When I saw the BBC documentary I realised what I'd been facilitating, and it broke my heart.'

By the end of the 1980s, Fayed had amassed dozens of assistants in his offices, many of whom had junior PAs. The amount of secretarial support he had was staggering, but very few of them were offering secretarial support, most were what Fayed called 'non-typists'; they were in his office because they were young, pretty and blonde.

Fayed would identify which of the women he wanted to come and work in his office by watching them on the cameras dotted around the store, by looking out for them on his store walks and by instructing his HR team to look out for attractive women. When Charlotte went to work in Harrods in 1989, she noticed that she was being photographed.

CHARLOTTE

Charlotte had been working in the luggage department for three days when she noticed a woman with a camera. She had come over to work at the store from New Zealand. Her mum had worked at Harrods decades earlier and spoken about what fun she'd had, living in London and working at such a prestigious place. It was an experience that Charlotte wanted for herself.

She was organising suitcases when a couple of managers at the store came to look round. 'I noticed they were taking pictures with a Polaroid camera, then they came up to me and asked my name. One of them wrote it on the back of the photograph, then they just walked off. I was only young and felt too nervous to ask them what they were doing, so I just tried to put it out of my mind. I guessed it must be for my work records.'

But later that day someone came to talk to her. Charlotte can't remember whether it was the same woman who had taken her photograph. The woman congratulated her and told her that she'd been promoted to work as one of Fayed's personal assistants.

'I was so pleased. It felt like a massive promotion. I remember telling my flatmate that night and he said, "Blimey, it's only Wednesday. You'll be running the place by Friday at this rate." It was an exciting thing to happen.'

On Thursday morning Charlotte reported in and was shown her desk but given little other information. 'I didn't know what I was supposed to do. No one spoke to me.' Then she was told that she needed a medical before she could work in the chairman's office. 'They said that the doctor was based in Harley Street, and told me how I should get there. The woman said I had to go straight away.

'When I got to the doctors I was expecting to do height, weight and blood pressure. It never even occurred to me that there might be more invasive tests than that. I was just going to be sitting in an office. Why would I need to have any other tests? Blood tests? Urine tests? Internal examinations? It was all so crazy, so I refused and left.'

When she got back from the appointment, she was told to go to the chairman's office straight away. 'I went running in there, I hadn't had time to take my coat off. There seemed to be this huge rush. I thought he was going to discuss what my new role at the company would be.

'I ran in and he said, "Why did you not have the tests?" I was so shocked I could hardly speak. I'd just walked back into the office and already the chairman of the whole company knew what had happened in my private medical. Why would he know? How would he know? He was really high up, he owned the whole place, why would he care? I was a nobody. None of it made any sense.'

Fayed told her that he thought she was special, and had a bright future, but there was no way in which he could employ her if she hadn't been through the medical. 'When

I went back to my desk, there was a note telling me to go straight back to the doctors.'

Charlotte went, against her instincts and better judgement, and she had the tests. When she arrived back at the store she was told to go to see the chairman. Once again, she didn't have time to remove her coat before she was bundled into his office. 'It was different this time. He was kind to start with, he said how proud he was that I'd had the tests and how pleased he was that I was all clear. I thought I'd misunderstood him – he couldn't have been given my results.'

He told her to take her coat off and relax. He put his hand on her thigh, and she sat there, nervously looking at his fingers and wondering how to make him move them. 'I shuffled in my seat, to move his hand, but it made things worse – he forced his hand up my skirt and was trying to tear my tights down. He grabbed at my breasts with the other hand. It was horrible. It seemed to come out of nowhere. He told me he'd look after me if I let him do what he wanted to.

'I didn't want his money, I wanted him to leave me alone. He ripped my blouse and laddered my tights. He was really rough and I was terrified. As soon as I could get away, I did. I ran back out through the office and ran out of the building. I got out onto the street and realised my coat was in his office, with my purse and keys in the pocket. I couldn't bear the thought of going back inside, so I walked to Shepherd's Bush, crying all the way. I sent a letter in the next day, saying the job wasn't for me and I was resigning.

'Someone from HR contacted me and said I needed to sign a form. It was an NDA. I signed it and that was the end of it.'

By the end of the 1980s, the roles for female employees at Harrods were well-defined; you were either someone who Fayed pressured to facilitate his actions or someone who was the target of his actions. Women had no choice about which category they were selected for, indeed they had no idea that Fayed was categorising them at all.

Between conquests he made women feel as vulnerable as he could by creating so many complicated 'no win' situations that no one knew quite how to act for fear of an unpredictable response.

One of these Catch-22 situations involved gift-giving. Fayed would offer women money and gifts for their attention. As soon as he'd made the offer, the woman was trapped. If she turned down his largesse, Fayed was deeply offended. He told women that Islamic tradition dictated that gift-giving and gift-receiving were an important rite of passage in social engagements.

As the Prophet Mohammed said, 'I shall accept the invitation even if I were invited to a meal of a sheep's trotter, and I shall accept the gift even if it were an arm or a trotter of a sheep.' So, it behoved you to accept a gift whether you wanted it or not.

But – and this is a pretty big but – if you accepted the gift, you were then beholden to him as he considered that he'd 'bought' your attention. You would, for example, be expected to accompany him on trips. His whole world and his outlook on life was transactional. He had given you the expensive handbag. Now what were you going to give him? This meant that for many women it was far easier simply to keep right out of his way rather than be offered a gift and find yourself offending him, or being in his debt. When Fayed did his store walks, women would hide – or be hidden by worried, older supervisors – until the chairman had passed.

Catch-22 situations were commonplace throughout Fayed's interactions with both men and women. They were a perfect tool to be employed by a boss who possessed a pathological need to win in every exchange and emerge from every contact feeling more powerful.

JOY

'I worked at Harrods in 1988, in my late teens, I guess I was seventeen or eighteen,' says Joy Mansfield. 'I remember that one of the women on the shop floor was black and we all made sure we hid her when Fayed did his walk around the store to prevent her being fired. We always hid the pretty girls, too. If he saw an attractive girl, she'd be moved up to work in the chairman's office, and I guess we all knew what that meant.

'As for the rest of us – we made sure we carried a spray and duster at all times and we'd clean furiously when his gang came round with their clipboards deciding who to fire. No one could relax – you were worried about being pestered by him or being fired by him. You were either too pretty or too ugly. You just couldn't win.'

Not that any of this bothered Fayed – he had plenty of women to choose from, and plenty more arriving all the time.

KATHERINE

Katherine was raped by Fayed in 1989 and has never spoken about it before. She told no one about the pain she suffered and the mental torture of being attacked by her boss. She still hasn't spoken to the police, nor has she instructed a lawyer or notified any of the victims' charities. 'That part of me feels dead. I buried it long, long ago. It's something I never mention. There's a gap on my CV where the time at Harrods should sit. I'd rather tell people that I spent those years in jail than tell them that I worked for that man.'

Katherine began working at the store as a trainee manager after her A levels. She describes herself as being 'overjoyed' when she was invited to join the store's scheme and further delighted when Fayed showed interest in her.

'I never expected to meet the man who owned the company, let alone be invited to a meeting with him so he could ask me how everything was going. I answered politely that everything was going well, and he said, "Good. Do you know what I have in this drawer?" He pointed to a desk drawer, and I said I didn't know.

'He opened it and it was full of boxes that he said contained Viagra. I just smiled. I didn't know what else to do. He then pulled out a huge black dildo and told me it was modelled on him, and did I think I could take it inside me? I just froze. I was on a management training course. I'd given up going to university for this chance. I couldn't ruin everything by running out of the room. I assumed he was testing me . . . putting me under pressure to see how I'd react.

'So I sat there, trying to remain professional and composed while this mad behaviour was going on all around me. Then he pulled out a pile of £5 and £10 notes, pulled open my blouse and shoved the money into my bra. He said he would pay me thousands more if I had sex with him. "I will have sex with you while you sit on this," he said, indicating the dildo. I was desperately trying to do up my blouse but two of the buttons had come off, so I held it together while he laughed at me.'

Katherine was three days into her job.

'The abuse continued from then onwards. I tried my hardest to carry out my job, but it was difficult. I was in a state of panic whenever a phone rang, in case it was one of his PAs telling me to go and see him. Even today I can't stand answering the phone. I associate telephones with abuse.'

She was nine months into her job when Fayed told her that she'd need to come to Paris with him on his private jet. 'I was so terrified about what would happen that I was physically sick the night before. My parents were proud of me for being the one chosen to accompany him on trips, and I didn't want to let them down. I loved that they were proud of me.'

She had dinner alone at the Ritz and was told to go up to a room afterwards that she was told was the business centre. It wasn't. It was Fayed's room and he was in there. 'The door locked and I was trapped. He made me drink something, I don't know what it was, but I don't remember anything after that. I woke up and I knew straight away that I had been raped. I was bleeding and sore. I think I was raped by the chairman but I think someone else raped me as well.

'I can't begin to tell you how much this has all affected my life. I can't cope with being out of my house, I don't trust anyone.'

Katherine says that a few years after the incident she tried to commit suicide by taking a whole bottle of sleeping pills that she'd been prescribed.

'I've had the most miserable life because of what he did to me,' she says.

Her time at Harrods came to an end when, three days after the trip, she was told that her employment had been terminated because she wasn't the right sort of personality to make it in management.

'They said they would give me a payoff if I signed an NDA. I said I didn't want to, and they said they knew where my parents lived and I needed to sign. So I did. But I didn't take the money.'

LOUISE

During her tenure at Harrods at the end of the 1980s Louise didn't work directly for the department store but for concessions – first Origins, then Tiffany's. Although she escaped personal assault from Fayed, she knew all about his reputation and saw the calculated methods used by security officials to dismiss women at will.

'Getting rid of people for no good reason was something he often did, either to remove them from the building or to demonstrate his absolute authority. I remember women accepting perfume samples from representatives eager to have their fragrances worn by sales staff. These women would place the samples in their bags, only to be accused of theft during end-of-day bag checks.' The security personnel knew these allegations were false, but objections were futile – the decision was irrevocable.

'When departments wrote off partial bottles of perfume to make way for new testers, we received these with explanatory notes from management so the guys on the door would know that the goods hadn't been stolen. Security might acknowledge this documentation and release you, or they might take the letter, rip it up and escort you to "the prison", where you'd be accused of theft. You never knew what response you'd get from the security guys.'

Louise joined during her gap year, to get experience in beauty marketing. She remembers the hierarchy represented by flowers: 'Managers wore red carnations, deputies had white ones. Only people wearing carnations could process refunds. We'd all be running around looking for these carnations before we were able to offer refunds.'

Louise says that many of the women Fayed was drawn to were on the graduate scheme, many from Oxbridge. 'I think he liked that – these beautiful English girls with cut-glass accents. He got a kick out of it. They were on the shop floor as part of their training; when you joined the management scheme, you needed that hands-on experience. Many thought they were beginning impressive careers and were reluctant to leave. None of us understood the extent of the abuse.'

Louise encountered Fayed several times: 'Once he patted my cheek, another time he pinched it quite hard. I was one of the lucky ones, though, I wasn't his type – I'm small with dark hair, and he preferred leggy blondes. Even though I say that, like everyone else I was anxious when he did his walks. We never knew who he would target next.'

The whole thing was appalling, but Louise does remember a woman called Barbara who worked hard to keep the young women safe. 'She'd move them all out of the way when Fayed came through on his inspections, and make sure the younger women weren't seen by him.

'If anything needed to be dropped into the office or there was any job to do that might involve contact with Fayed, Barbara would always go herself rather than risk him seeing the other girls. She was quite old at the time and had been at Harrods for years. I heard that she died in service. She was an incredible woman. You wonder how many women were saved because of her. When I think back now, I think of her lugging Fayed's bags around for him, so the younger girls didn't have to do it.'

But Louise says it's the unlimited power of the security officers that remains most vivid in her memory: 'I'd never known anything like it then and I haven't come across it since. They could do whatever they wanted. It was like being in China or North Korea. They could march you off the shop floor to a prison-like room downstairs. You didn't need to do anything unlawful. Just looking at them the wrong way could land you in trouble.

'I remember someone being followed by security all weekend because Fayed wanted to know whether the woman had a boyfriend. How can that be right? How can there be a situation where a young woman is followed around all weekend by two security guards on the instruction of their boss? He was a horrible man who brought misery wherever he went.'

CLAIRE

Claire has quite a different story to tell about Fayed, which is far removed from the image of the man that has emerged from every other interview I've done. Her experiences may go some way to explaining how he was able to fool so many people for so much of the time.

Claire is British, and her ex-husband was an influential, well-connected surgeon from Kuwait. They were something of a 'power couple'. They had been invited to spend time on *Nabila*, the incredible 280-foot yacht owned by Saudi billionaire Adnan Khashoggi, Fayed's former brother-in-law. The yacht was named after Khashoggi's daughter, and at the time it was the largest private yacht in the world, with five decks and eleven suites. Khashoggi ended up selling it to Donald Trump in the late 1980s, but while he had it he liked to party, and at one of these parties were Claire and her husband, along with Fayed, who had resumed his friendship with Khashoggi, and an array of other friends.

'I know this doesn't fit with what a lot of other women have said, but I found him to be charming and fun. I loved his company and never felt threatened or hassled by him. I spent quite a lot of time with him on that holiday. I can speak Arabic and was talking in Arabic to him. He was helping me with my pronunciations and laughing along with me when I got things wrong. He genuinely was fun, and I liked him a lot. I met him in Nice, then in Puerto Banús. There were lots of girls hanging around, in the way that billionaires always have lots of pretty girls hanging around. But these weren't young girls or hired for the occasion. They were friends.

'Everyone was having fun. Nothing inappropriate happened. We had a few drinks and a bit of a laugh. I remember going off to the casino one time when we met in Monte Carlo. He had loads of his friends there.

He was extremely family-orientated, not on the make at all.

'There were business meetings taking place and my husband was making connections for them. It was all very good-humoured. Egyptians can be very rowdy. The language is guttural. You think they are shouting at one another, but it's just that the language is aggressive. They talk over one another all the time. Once you get used to Arabic society, you know there's nothing offensive in it – it just sounds aggressive to us.

'I saw them again in Monte Carlo and Marbella, and don't have a bad word to say about him. I met him maybe three or four times, and I know that my ex-husband stayed in touch with them and continued to work with them.

'I think Fayed was quite fascinated by me and would come over and see me and ask me to talk to him in my Egyptian accent. He was really in awe that I had learned to speak Arabic and impressed by me for making the effort. I think he wanted to encourage me because so few English people speak Middle Eastern languages.

'I'd say things and he'd laugh and gently take the mickey out of me. It was nothing offensive. They are very handsy in that nationality, always touching and hugging each other. But they mean no offence. None was meant and none was taken. Arrogance is quite an Egyptian thing, and all the posturing of being wealthy, but that's just what it's like in that country. Every country is different.

'He certainly wasn't a sex fiend. He wasn't a pushy bloke, not some predator. I spent time alone with him on many occasions. There was never a problem. He was a nice guy. If he offered you jewels, money and handbags then – sure – he probably wanted something in return. He's from a very transactional society, but I find it very difficult to match up the man I met with the man talked about today.'

10

SILENCE AND SUBMISSION

HARRODS IN THE 90s

'A man of that age should not be mixing with young girls, offering them lifts in his Rolls-Royce and chauffeur-driven limo, and buying them presents before inviting them to his house. How is any of that appropriate?'

James, a former teacher at West Heath School, which Fayed bought in 1998

PATSY

Patsy is a no-nonsense woman who says she treated Fayed 'like the big child he is' when she worked for him as a personal assistant in the mid-1990s. 'He wanted to be treated like a God, and he loved the way everyone bowed and curtseyed before him, but somehow I got away with treating him like a normal person, and telling him off when needed. I'm not conventionally attractive – I'm a pretty solid five-foot-one German woman, and that helped.'

Patsy was employed in Fayed's office after a stressful period working as a court stenographer, taking down an accurate account of the day's proceedings. She said she needed something lighter and a little more varied than spending everyday transcribing. She was also finding the whole thing depressing; sitting down for hours every day and listening to the gross details of heinous crimes wasn't doing her mental health any good. She saw an advert for a job in Harrods as an executive personal assistant and decided that was exactly what she needed.

'I was called in to Harrods and met a woman who worked in HR, as far as I remember. She didn't ask me very sophisticated questions, just ran through my CV and said someone would be in touch. I was expecting her to quiz me on the fact that I hadn't worked in retail and hadn't been a PA before. I was prepared for all these complicated questions, but there weren't any. I went home and was called back in a few days later. This time I was told I was going to meet the chairman because I'd be working directly for him.

'When I went for the interview, I found him charming and engaging. I told him about my role in court, and he seemed genuinely impressed. I said that nothing fazed me after listening to criminal trials for years and that I'd seen it all. He wanted to know about cases I'd seen and showed real interest in my work. He said that I might see things working for Harrods that were controversial but I should always keep quiet, and that what happened at Harrods, stayed at Harrods.

'Then he asked me who was the most dangerous man I'd seen in court, and he wanted to know a lot of detail about the crimes I'd seen. I know that sounds like a red flag now, but I definitely didn't think this was odd at the time. People were always interested. His interest didn't seem out of the ordinary. Now, when I think back, I can see that he was fascinated by the criminals I mentioned, but back then I thought it was lovely that he was paying me such attention.'

Patsy was told that she had the job. She explained that she could start in three months, after her notice period.

'He didn't like that. He wanted me to start straight away. I must have had half a dozen calls from the women in his office telling me I'd have to break my contract and come into Harrods immediately, and if there was any trouble he'd sort it out.

'I said I didn't want to do that, and they said that I couldn't come and work for him then. The tone of calls was always, "Do you not realise who we're dealing with here? This is Mohamed Fayed." I ended up serving two of my three months' notice, then went to work at Harrods after that.'

Patsy was in her early thirties when she took the job and recognises that she was an 'actual typist' rather than a 'non-typist'. She recalls attending an initiation programme welcoming her to Harrods, then she went to the offices where there were lots of incredibly beautiful women swanning around, all dressed similarly, heavily made-up, perfect hair. She joked to her friends that it was like Stepford Wives, and that there was 'something creepy about it'.

'I mean the women were all lovely, I really liked them, but they all dressed in the way that Fayed liked his women to dress. Can you imagine that? I've never known anything like it, before or since. It was a very strange place full of terrified women who wanted to conform.'

Patsy went to her desk and tried to work out what needed to be done. She says that no one had much of a clue what was required, and everyone was waiting to be told what their jobs were for the day. In the end she went to HR to say there seemed to be nothing to do. They told her to relax and settle in.

'Over the coming months, I started taking over a bit and acting as a funnel – finding out what needed to be done and passing that along to the women in the office. I never had any sexual abuse from the boss. We never had that sort of relationship. I think he saw me as smart and efficient, nothing like the women he fancied.

'He was very odd, though, there's no question about that. I thought we might end up being friends of some sort, but we weren't – not by a long way. I don't think he had friends – he wasn't interested in anyone but himself, and the sooner you realised that the better.

'He was very inappropriate at times. He waved a dildo at me and told me I could borrow it any time I wanted, and would often present me with little tins of sweets that he told me were Viagra. He asked me to go and buy him a sex doll once, then howled with laughter and said he was joking. I remember one occasion when he handed me a bra that he said he'd found in his office and wanted to know whether it was mine. He said he knew I'd been using his office to have sex and wanted to know whether I was a lesbian.'

Patsy says she told him not to be ridiculous and that he needed to grow up.

'When I hear all the accounts today about how he'd punish anyone who crossed him, I'm surprised he didn't turn on me, but he didn't. He'd just send me away when I was annoying him.'

She says she had absolutely no idea that he was abusing the secretaries she worked with. 'There wasn't much chatter in the offices because we knew the whole place was bugged. The fact that he recorded everything didn't bother me at the time because I assumed it was all for security. I knew he had a colourful background and suspected he was very nervous about his personal security, so it seemed fine that he took steps to ensure his own safety. But it did stop people from talking, and now we know the truth about him, I think we all realise how damaging it was not to be able to confide in other people.'

She was aware of the fast turnover of women, though. 'Women would come and go from the offices and there were always new girls starting and others disappearing. Now I wonder if I should have been more aware of what was going on, but I thought women were being moved from department to department. I knew he was attracted to the women; he made that clear. I didn't think it went any further than that. I never dealt with any paperwork relating to the claims of sexual abuse.

'The only falling-out I had with him was when I wanted to leave because I was starting a family. He told me I was disloyal and he'd never get over the way I had let him down. He said he'd never speak to me again . . . and he didn't.

'He was a very odd man, that's for sure.'

AMY

It was 1993, and a twenty-one-year-old Canadian woman was working on the shop floor at Harrods when she was hand-picked by the chairman to be one of his many personal assistants, based at his Park Lane property.

She had to undergo a medical, of course, which was undignified enough in itself, but she was then forced to suffer the embarrassment of being told the results by Fayed. He explained that she had a small infection and presented her with the medication to cure it. Indignity piled upon indignity.

Once the infection was cured, he made his move, grabbing her from behind the head, pulling her in and kissing her. He tried to stick his tongue down her throat as she wriggled and struggled to break free. But it would get worse. In October 1993 Fayed told Amy that she'd have to accompany him on a work trip to Villa Windsor, his mansion in the west of Paris. It was there that he tried to rape her.

She described the click of the door, the smell of alcohol, him pouncing on her, his hands everywhere, being pinned down, the weight of this man intent on raping her. 'It was the most terrifying thing I can remember in my life,' she recalls. 'Awful.'

But what's peculiar about Amy's story is that she made a random reference to her mother, telling Fayed, 'If my mother knew what was going on, she'd be horrified.'

This led to him stopping abruptly. He put a towel around his waist and left the room. There was something about Amy mentioning her mother that caused him to halt his assault. A chink in his armour. Perhaps a flashback to losing his own mother, or maybe her comment was enough for Fayed to remember, briefly, that here was a real human being he was dealing with, not just a character in the glamorous tale of Mohamed Al-Fayed.

REBECCA

Rebecca Loos, the woman who alleged in 2003 that she'd had an affair with David Beckham, also worked as an assistant for Fayed. She started in the offices as a filing clerk and general administrator, and says she enjoyed the role and the people she worked with, but there was one issue she had to contend with while she was there: Fayed.

She hadn't met him in her time working at the store, then one morning a rumour spread through the office that he'd be coming to pay a visit. 'I thought, that sounds exciting,' said Loos.

But no one else in the office found the prospect at all thrilling as they quickly moved to hide the younger, more attractive girls from him.

'My female colleague said to me, "Don't let him see you, Rebecca, hide, he likes pretty young girls. He has an apartment down the road where he takes them. You do not want to get involved, so make sure he doesn't see you." She was an older lady – we used to have lunch together every day – and she just said, "Make sure he doesn't see you. Hide behind the filing cabinets when he comes."

'So I hid, never saw him, never met him. And that's why I believe all the stories in the media today. I just can't believe it has taken this long to come out.'

Such was the fear of Fayed and what he was capable of, that older women in the office were hiding younger women away from him.

Later on, long after she had left Harrods, when she was twenty-six years old, Loos talked publicly about her alleged affair with Beckham and found herself in the headlines for months with her lurid, colourful stories about their assignations and the revelation of the hundreds of messages he'd sent her. She earned herself over £1 million from interviews and TV appearances associated with the story, and became a household name. But Fayed was not happy with her revelations and moved quickly to make clear his displeasure.

Loos had planned to attend a champagne reception at Harrods with Max Clifford, the PR svengali working for Fayed who was also masterminding the media attention garnered by Loos's revelations. But once Fayed found out she was coming, he intervened and ordered that her invitation be withdrawn. Fayed said he'd been friends with the Beckhams for years, and Victoria had opened the Harrods January sale in 2002. He did not want to seem disloyal.

'I told Max Clifford I couldn't have her here,' said Fayed. 'David Beckham is a good friend and a good client, I told Max "no".'

WEST HEATH SCHOOL

One of the most troubling developments in the Fayed story concerns a school that Fayed bought. He purchased West Heath School – attended by Diana, Princess of Wales – in late May 1998, almost a year after her death in Paris. He paid $4 million for the school (around £2.4 million by 1998 exchange rate), and he said the school would change its raison d'être and serve children who had suffered physical and sexual abuse or had mental disabilities and chronic illnesses.

His rationale for buying the school was to protect the place where Diana had enjoyed herself (she said it was the happiest time of her life). But there were rumblings about what was really going on there, and concern about what Fayed's real interest was in a school full of the sort of well-spoken girls and young women that he'd shown such a penchant for when he spotted them on the sales floor. But, obviously, these were children, in a school environment, where they should have been safe.

James,* a former teacher at the school, says, 'I always thought it was odd. I know that's easy to say in hindsight, but I did. I found it creepy and odd. Fayed would come to the school sometimes and it would be the big Mohamed show, like when he came with celebrities [he turned up with Madonna in June 2010].

'But there were other times he'd come and just stroll in alone and start talking to the girls. No one seemed to stop him because he'd saved the school from closing. He was free to wander around and do whatever he liked. I never thought that was right. I thought the headmistress should have been walking round with him, but she might not even have realised that he was there. He seemed to be able to turn up unannounced.

'I know he'd saved the school, but even parents aren't allowed to walk in and walk around.'

I ask James whether he suspected that Fayed was trying to recruit girls.

'There's no question that he was. I know he told girls he could get them jobs, and he'd give them things from Harrods. He invited a couple of the girls to his house. I spoke to another teacher and we went to talk to a head of department at the school about it. They said that it was fine and we shouldn't worry, but it wasn't fine. I knew it wasn't. I carried on worrying about it.

'He shouldn't have been there. Benefactor or not, a man of that age should not be mixing with young girls, offering them lifts in his Rolls-Royce and chauffeur-driven limo, and buying them presents before inviting them to his house. How is any of that appropriate?'

When all of the information about Fayed came out after his death, James says he 'literally punched the wall in anger and frustration. I knew it was wrong. I should have done more.'

James put me in touch with a woman who worked at the school, but not as a teacher. Jessica* says she knows of a girl who was abused by Fayed while attending West Heath School.

'There's a girl who was definitely abused,' Jessica tells me, 'but I couldn't get her to go to the police, and she refused to tell anyone at the school but me. I guess that because I wasn't part of the teaching staff, she felt safer telling me. She was nervous and crying. Fayed had invited her to Harrods and attacked her in the boardroom. He didn't manage to rape her, but he tore her clothes and he hurt her. She kicked him and he slapped her and called her an ungrateful animal.

'He said that he would pull the money out of the school and close it down if she said anything. He told her that her parents would be told about how she had behaved and all the school would know that she was the one who closed the school down. She was terrified. She felt like she was to blame, and nothing I said would calm her down.'

As in so many of the stories related here, Fayed took advantage of the people who were most vulnerable. By telling the girls that he would close the place down if they spoke out, he tapped into their fears about letting down all their friends, their parents and the school.

Jessica says that she has been made aware of other girls who were attacked by Fayed and at least one who was raped. She reported her findings to her lawyers and plans to contact the Harrods Survivors support group on their behalf. 'When I spoke to lawyers, they put me on to some lawyers working with a lot of the victims, and they were already aware of the claims. They said they had been contacted by girls who were at the school and by the relatives of one girl who committed suicide. The family are convinced it's because of what she went through with Fayed. I know they are also investigating that he fathered a love child with an underaged girl. I don't know any more details. I don't work at the school any more, and I'm very glad that Fayed is dead.'

Four days after the BBC documentary, West Heath School issued their only comments on the allegations – 'We have no further information other than what is currently in the news' – adding, 'We do not tolerate abuse or harassment in any form.' My requests for information have been met with a referral to these statements.

ANNE-MARIE

Many of the women abused by Fayed came from abroad, in many cases travelling to the UK for the sole purpose of working in the celebrated store. It meant that when things went wrong, they were on their own – confused, hurt and miles from home.

Anne-Marie Kruk travelled from the capital of Australia to the British capital to take up a job at Harrods, but as she boarded a plane in Canberra for the bright lights of London, she had no idea of the fate that awaited her.

She recalls her excitement when she started work at the store. 'There were celebrities who came to visit. The windows were amazing. It was a really magical place for me and getting a job there, it felt like a dream.'

Anne-Marie is one of a growing group of Australian women who have come forward to say they were abused by Fayed. In March 2025 the Australian channel Nine News broadcast a *60 Minutes* TV documentary about women from that country who were abused by Fayed, a programme similar in tone to the BBC documentary about him broadcast in the UK the previous year.

Anne-Marie worked as a receptionist in store approvals, the department run by Kelly Walker-Duncalf, described by several interviewees as 'the second most powerful person in the business'. Walker-Duncalf was glamorous, sophisticated – and very close to Fayed. She was responsible for ensuring that all the 'right' people came to work at Harrods. Another way to phrase this might be, she was responsible for ensuring that the business was staffed by women whom Fayed would find attractive. A *Dispatches* investigation called *Delivered to a Predator: Al Fayed's Fixer* also found Walker-Duncalf to be at the centre of Fayed's operation. Both the presenter Cathy Newman and I believe that she made it possible for Fayed to behave as he did. Walker-Duncalf found women for him. Whether she was complicit to any degree or knew of Fayed's abuse are matters for the police to investigate, but what may be said for present purposes is that she was the means by which many victims came to his attention. She literally delivered his victims to him. Walker-Duncalf didn't return any of my calls or messages, but her lawyers have denied that she assisted Fayed in his criminality: 'She did not, at any stage, facilitate or enable any of Al-Fayed's crimes.'

Anne-Marie was one such victim; she was exactly the sort of woman that Fayed would find attractive. She was a pretty, blonde twenty-one-year-old, and it didn't take long before she caught the chairman's eye and was invited to go and meet him.

Walker-Duncalf told Anne-Marie she was 'lucky' that the chairman wanted to meet her. Anne-Marie met Fayed and was offered a job in his office as an assistant. After accepting the role, she was informed she'd be required to undergo a medical examination by doctors on Harrods's payroll, her first-ever internal gynaecological examination.

'They didn't need to know my STD profile. They didn't need to do a hormone check. They didn't need to do a swab that had absolutely nothing to do with what I was doing on a daily basis. They were doing it because he was someone who had an obsession with hygiene in general, and I think that extended to every part of you,' she said. 'And because he was a serial sexual abuser, it was obvious that he was doing it to make sure that if he decided to do something with you, that you were clean.'

Anne-Marie said it was after the medical that Fayed's sexual assaults and harassment started. 'He would talk to you about how he could help you in your career and then, you know, give you some money and say, "Go and buy yourself something nice." And so that was kind of how the grooming process started. And then it evolved from there. It was after I'd had my medical that the chairman started to kiss me on the mouth, not on the cheek. Or starting to put his hand down my top and squeeze, put his hand on my leg.'

This pattern of unwanted touching and harassment continued relentlessly for eight months, with Fayed taking every opportunity to assault her. The situation escalated dramatically when she was summoned to Fayed's Park Lane apartment. There, he attempted to rape her.

'It made me feel cheap, it made me feel dirty, and I didn't know what to do. I just remember he had this really puckered mouth. He was an old man. And I remember thinking, "This is so gross." And he tried to force me down. I knew that if I made him really angry, then I'd lose my job.

'When you put all of the pieces together you realise that, within a corporate context, you were kind of being sold into being a sex object without your knowledge,' she says. 'The fact that that took place within what you thought was a legitimate company, it's so difficult to get your head around it.'

Anne-Marie fought him off and resigned from her job at Harrods, but the trauma of the attempted rape has remained with her.

'You were the least powerful up against the most powerful.'

Christmas, capitalism and cartoons. Outside Harrods with Mickey Mouse, waiting for Father Christmas. Fayed loved to display his playful side, but his smiles and dressing-up were the public face of an evil man.

Fayed's faithful. With two of his doormen in 1987, two years after buying Harrods.

Above: **Walking with the late Queen.** With Queen Elizabeth II, 1988. Fayed's brief moment inside the royal circle, before the doors quietly closed again.

Top right: **The Windsors' shadow.** At his Paris mansion, once occupied by the Duke and Duchess of Windsor. Fayed was always drawn to royalty, even the exiled kind.

Right: **The butcher of Terminal 3.** Opening a Harrods Food Hall at Heathrow, 1990. A suit, a butcher's hat and a global ambition: Fayed took Harrods everywhere – even to Departures.

Polo, protocol and PR. Presenting a gift to Prince Charles, 1989. Fayed often courted the Establishment, even as it declined to fully admit him.

Above: **Driving the message home.**
Dressed as a Harrods carriage driver
in green, waving beside a Christmas coach.
Behind him, a model shark named 'Tiny' –
a not-so-subtle jab at rival Tiny Rowland.
Once someone had upset Fayed, he never
forgot it.

Right: **Fergie, fashion and fundraising.**
With Sarah Ferguson at a *Vogue* charity
event at Harrods, 1991. Fayed knew the
value of royal association, even when it
came with baggage.

**The Harrods throne
room.** In his office
in Knightsbridge,
the heart of his
empire, where cash
and confrontation
were daily tools of
the trade.

Country house. Fayed's beautiful estate near Oxted, Surrey. This quintessential country retreat was revealed as the location for numerous attacks on women.

A gift to the Met. Fayed was the first businessman to donate a patrol car to the Metropolitan Police. Touted as public-spirited generosity, it was later overshadowed by questions about his relationships with the force.

A princess and her host. With Princess Diana at a Harrods charity dinner, February 1996. Fayed was so obsessed with the princess that he sent her hampers and gifts, and offered her anything she wanted. He was desperate to pair her with his eldest son, Dodi.

Pioneers. Announcing Europe's first full-time professional women's football team at Fulham FC. Fayed was lauded for his commitment to the women's game, but since his death stories of his abuse of several of the players have emerged.

Crowning glories. With model Michelle G and a discounted diamond coronet to mark the opening of the Harrods sale, 1998. Cher missed the event due to the death of her ex-husband Sonny Bono, but Fayed never passed up a chance to be close to a glamorous woman and occupy centre stage.

Pharaohs and faux grandeur. The Egyptian escalator at Harrods, designed by Fayed to honour his heritage. He once said, 'When I die, I want to be mummified and buried under the Harrods Egyptian escalator in a glass pyramid.'

Veneer of respectability. Seated like a king at his polished table in his private office suite at Harrods, 1999. But behind the opulence, cracks were beginning to form – an ITV documentary and a biography by Tom Bower had just been released, accusing him of attacking women. For all the noise, he walked away seemingly untouched by the revelations.

Above: **Butcher and showman**. Dressed as a butcher for the launch of Mo's Diner, Harrods, 2002. Fayed always believed that selling sausages was about theatre as much as taste.

Right: **Security, screens and conspiracy.** John Macnamara was a former senior police officer who led Fayed's security team and covered up much of the abuse that took place.

Above: **Selling the dream.** Fayed with Liz Hurley and Arun Nayar at Harrods, 2005, for the launch of Elizabeth Hurley Beach. Celebrity sparkle was always part of the Fayed retail formula.

Above: **Yachts, wealth and watchfulness.** On his yacht *Sakara* in Saint-Tropez, 2009. He sailed in luxury, always pursued by questions, cameras – and his past. He abused several women on the yacht, including Melissa Price, an ambassador's daughter.

Trial by media. Outside the High Court, 2007, as the inquest into Diana and Dodi began. A man used to managing the narrative, now at the mercy of it.

Above: **Pop royalty at a private school.** With Madonna at West Heath, Princess Diana's alma mater, in 2010. Fayed bought the school in 1998 and went out of his way to impress the pupils, offering them trips to Harrods and outings in his chauffeur-driven car.

Top right: **Family premiere, public stage.** With sons Omar and Karim at the *Spectre* premiere, 2015. Fayed's public appearances often blended showbiz, dynasty and image control.

Right: **In the company of Heini.** With his wife Heini Wathén in Paris, 2016. A rare moment of quiet glamour in a life usually lived at full volume.

Caught in the frame. Hands outstretched, eyes on the camera: 'Who, me?' Fayed often played innocent, even when no one was buying the act.

What has also remained with her is the role that Walker-Duncalf played in her treatment at Harrods. 'She would have sent hundreds of girls up to his office in the ten years she was there. She even asked me to look out for attractive candidates so that she could recommend them to him. She focused on attractive blondes. I mean, even all of us in the store approvals office were blonde. And there was a board up with loads of Polaroid photos of women on it. She'd take the pictures up to show the chairman.'

GEMMA

Fayed approached Gemma and told her she'd need to accompany him to Paris, to Villa Windsor, his home in the Bois de Boulogne. It would be a work trip to attend meetings at his fourteen-room mansion. Gemma would get to see the place in all its splendour – the gleaming marble floors and ornate chandeliers, the antique Louis XV and Louis XVI furnishings, the sweeping staircases. It should have been a treat, but Gemma feared the worst.

She'd already endured months of grabbing and groping before the trip, so she decided to record everything secretly, for her own security.

The first sign that things were awry came when they arrived in Paris and Fayed insisted that he keep hold of her passport, meaning that she was unable to leave the country. Then, on the first night, Fayed entered her room uninvited. Gemma recorded what unfolded, as he pressured her into 'making love' with him. When she refused, he said, 'Well, why did you come then?', as if she was somehow complicit by agreeing to go on a work trip with him and should have known what would happen.

Fayed left her room and Gemma tried to calm herself down. She'd finally started to drift off to sleep when he returned, wearing a short silk dressing gown, open at the front, more determined than ever. He got into her bed and attacked her in 'the worst way possible'. He then instructed her to go and wash herself with Dettol. The disinfectant had been placed in the bathroom in advance of her arrival, so Gemma knew the whole thing was pre-planned. He had taken her to Paris to abuse her.

Gemma was one of the women who appeared in the BBC documentary. After the attack, she made a sexual harassment complaint to the Harrods HR department when she returned to London and was waved away with a derisory financial offer. She told them that she'd recorded her interactions with Fayed, and they responded that the money would only be forthcoming if she signed an NDA and destroyed the evidence she'd accumulated – her recordings of Fayed, along with transcripts and other documents.

Gemma did this, wanting the whole episode to be over.

She left Harrods and thought her ordeal had come to an end, but no, Fayed bombarded her with calls. She says that some days she was receiving twenty-five to thirty calls from him. He sent his security personnel to pick Gemma up and bring her back to work, and he told the Harrods doctors to phone her and tell her that she had lost her mind and needed to come back for medical help.

'I ended up having to move house and change my phone number and sell my car just to get rid of him,' she said.

11

BEYOND HARRODS

FULHAM FC AND OTHER HUNTING GROUNDS

'If some stupid fans don't understand and appreciate such a gift, they can go to hell.'

Fayed, to *Vanity Fair*, after he unveiled a statue of Michael Jackson at the ground

On 29 May 1997 Fayed stood in the middle of Fulham Football Club's pitch, wrapped in the club's scarf, and announced: 'I have a football club. I consider myself more British than the British royal family.'

He grinned from ear-to-ear as he made a show of kicking a football in front of the assembled journalists, talking animatedly of his great love for the national game and how British he felt now he owned Fulham. One did get the sense that the purchase was all about him taking another step towards proving how British he was. It was as if everything he did was in pursuit of the citizenship that he craved so much.

He had tried everything to get citizenship, and he hated the fact that it had not been bestowed; it represented rejection – confirmation that despite his wealth, his properties and his power, he remained an outsider. The boy from the Gomrok slum who'd gazed longingly at the Alexandria Yacht Club was now the billionaire who could buy Harrods but couldn't secure a British passport. Psychiatrist Maurice Eisenbruch coined the term 'cultural bereavement' to describe how immigrants often experience a profound sense of loss for their homeland that manifests as an idealisation of the host culture. Fayed's obsession with becoming British, his immense wealth and influence notwithstanding, reflects this psychological phenomenon.

No one could accuse Fayed at not working hard enough at a British identity. He bought a 14th-century castle in Scotland, he owned Harrods, he oversaw the creation of a Scottish tartan in the name of his Highland fortress, he maintained a fleet of Rolls-Royces, and sponsored both the Royal Windsor Horse Show and polo, the 'sport of kings'. He also financed *Chariots of Fire*, that quintessentially British film about British Olympic triumph, and supported British fashion labels.

All that was missing was football, so he snapped up a lovely club on the banks of the Thames in one of the more salubrious areas of London, and promised to invest £30 million and bring Premier League football to Craven Cottage within five years.

It seemed like inflamed rhetoric at the time but, to be fair, Fayed was true to his word. The team started their inexorable rise from the third tier to the Premier League, where they finished in thirteenth place in the 2001/02 season. Fayed also bought a training ground and created the first full-time professional women's team in Europe. In 2010 Fulham reached the final of the Europa League for the first time. His period in charge was a great success . . . on the pitch.

He moved quickly to bring two of the biggest names in the game on board, with Kevin Keegan appointed as COO and Ray 'Butch' Wilkins as manager. A few weeks later he signed Fulham's first £1 million player, Paul Peschisolido (Baroness Karren Brady's husband).

Along the way, Fayed injected his unique sense of theatre. Among the most memorable of his changes to the ground was a statue of Michael Jackson that appeared outside the ground after the pop star had accompanied him to watch a match. He hired a witch to curse Chelsea, Fulham's local rivals, and frequently dressed as a pharaoh at club events. He once tried to sell 'magic Egyptian energy bars' to Fulham fans, claiming they would boost their energy levels.

Then, there were the famous visitors to Craven Cottage. He flew in actors like Sylvester Stallone, Tony Curtis and Kevin Costner to sit in the crowd, as well as Daniel Radcliffe, Hugh Grant and supermodel Naomi Campbell. Up in the stands were footballing legends George Best, Pelé and Maradona, while Elton John represented pop superstardom, all of which helped make the Cottage feel like an extraordinary and exciting place to be. Crowds were bigger, players were paid more and were more successful, and the coaching was better. Soon enough the results came in. Fulham were flying.

But off the pitch it was far from extraordinary and exciting.

AMANDA

Amanda* was on the fringes of the Fulham women's team and keen to become the best player she could be. 'Women's football was growing,' she says, 'and Fayed had become a bit of a hero by setting up the first professional women's side. I trained really hard and did everything I could to impress people.'

Amanda does not want to reveal her age, but she was very young at the time, still at school while training at Craven Cottage. 'I remember talking to Mum about how much I was enjoying it. Neither my mum nor dad are football fans so I don't think they understood, but they were supportive.' She says she told her mum that Fayed would be visiting the training ground and her mum said, 'Be nice to him, make sure you stand out from the crowd.'

When Fayed walked in, Amanda says that the place went quiet and everyone stopped what they were doing. She was nervous, but remembered her mum's words, so she bounded up to him, put out her hand to shake his and said, 'Hello, I'm Amanda and I'm hoping to get into the first team soon.' Little did she know that this was manna from heaven for Fayed. A pretty young woman who wanted something that he could get for her.

'He came over to me later and invited me to come to his apartment to discuss my role at Fulham and whether he could help me to make it into the first team. I was so excited. He told me that someone from the club would drive me in, and he'd make sure I got back safely.' Amanda was picked up by a big black car later that day, driven by someone she didn't recognise. She'd been told that someone from the club would drive her, but this was a complete stranger.

'When I got to his apartment he didn't even mention football. All he wanted to know was whether I had a boyfriend, had I lost my virginity, had I ever kissed a man? He was sitting right next to me and had his hand on my thigh, stroking my leg as we talked. He said I had good legs and they'd be perfect for playing football. He asked me to show them to him.' Amanda was wearing her tracksuit and had no desire to remove the trousers. She remembers she felt awkward and confused.

'I can get you a place in the team,' Fayed told her. 'I own the club, I can do whatever I like. I need to see your legs to see whether they're strong enough.' Amanda took down her tracksuit trousers and says that Fayed became like an animal, reaching out to try and touch her legs.

'He asked me to bend over, and he told me to take my knickers off. I realised that was all wrong and ran for the door, but my tracksuit bottoms were round my ankles and I was struggling to pull them up while running. I got to the door and it was locked. I banged and banged on it with all my might. I'd just about got my trousers pulled up when I heard a voice on the other side, so I screamed and kicked at the door. I was sure Fayed was going to come running after me, but he stayed in his seat, laughing at me. The door opened and I ran out.'

RONNIE

Ronnie Gibbons, Fulham's former women's captain, has spoken about her experiences with Fayed. She was sexually assaulted by him in 2000 and 2001, the first time when she was twenty years old. She'd been told to come to a meeting at Harrods, to speak to Fayed's children about football. She was happy to do this, as spreading the word about the women's game was something she took seriously.

When she arrived at Harrods she asked Fayed where his children were. They couldn't make it, he said. This immediately struck her as odd, since the whole point in her being there was to meet the children. Instead, he told her to come and sit next to him. In that locked room she was forcibly kissed, groped and made to sit on Fayed's knee.

When she finally got away, she said nothing about what she had endured. She didn't speak out about the abuse because she didn't want to prejudice the future of the women's team. She told The Athletic website, 'I just felt a huge responsibility on my shoulders because we'd just turned professional. Everything internally was screaming at me, "Ronnie, you need to leave," but I couldn't because I would be to blame for all these women losing their jobs and Fulham Ladies going down the pan.

'I couldn't allow anything to happen to me, but at the same time, I couldn't just run for the hills, which is what I wanted to do.'

'I never worked at the club,' says security officer Biggie, 'but I'm aware that there were complaints. They were similar complaints to the ones being made at Harrods – that he was trying to grope girls. I found it quite hard to believe that it was going on at Fulham. These women were leading players – they could easily have spoken to the press and got him in trouble. There was always a feeling that he was a bit of a loose cannon at Fulham.

'There were journalists at the club for press conferences, so what he was doing was much riskier. I guess he knew the players wouldn't say anything because he might fold the team or throw them out of it, but I still thought it was odd that he was turning up there and inviting them to meet him. I know the club ended up developing a system where they made sure a male member of staff was always with the women when the boss was around. He was mad, though – these women were in the papers and on TV. He was taking a huge risk by messing with them.' That certainly applied to Ronnie Gibbons, who was not only captain of her club but also an international player for the Republic of Ireland.

Both Ronnie and Amanda say that the BBC documentary brought all the hurt and pain rushing back. 'It had never quite gone away,' says Ronnie. 'A glimpse of someone who looks like him, the mention of Harrods or even certain smells have always reminded me of him.' Her interest in the sport waned, so she handed in her captain's armband and stopped playing football at twenty-five. 'I feel very sad that I had to do that, but I had no choice.'

Amanda says the same: 'I didn't stay in football long after that . . . it didn't hold anything like the same joy for me. At training I'd dread him coming down, and I was never selected for the first team. I was actually pleased not to be selected, that would have brought me back into contact with him. I stopped going to training and slowly drifted away from the club.' She is reluctant to talk about whether she went to the police to report what happened. She says simply, 'I tried, but they weren't really interested, so I left the police station.' Three of the Fulham players I have interviewed also went to the police to report Fayed, but again nothing ever happened.

One other story that arose after I talked to players at Fulham FC concerns Kevin Keegan, the former Liverpool, Hamburg and England star, who was brought in to coach the Fulham men's team. Keegan left Fulham when he became England manager in 1999, citing the difficulties of coaching club and country at the same time. Fayed said he would let Keegan go because he was a patriot. 'I've given you my Keegan,' he quipped at the time, 'now can I have my British passport.'

But there are stories that it was all much more complicated than that, and that Fayed and Keegan fell out because the fax machine that Fayed had given to Keegan for home use when he started at the club stopped working. Rather than call the club, Keegan went to a local repair centre, where a bugging device was found in the machine.

Once Keegan realised that Fayed possessed the ability to listen in on everything he and others said within the safety of his home, he decided to go.

Keegan could not be reached for comment.

Fayed was creating opportunities everywhere to meet attractive women. Those in his employ were vulnerable and there for the taking, and by buying a football club and setting up the first professional women's section, and then a girls' school, he pulled more women and girls into his orbit.

He systematically created opportunities to isolate and abuse these women wherever he went. His properties, businesses and even his charitable efforts weren't just status symbols, financial investments or apparent philanthropy – they were elaborate traps specifically designed to give him access to females.

One of the ways in which he used his homes to abuse was by hiring attractive young women as domestic staff. Barrow Green Court, Fayed's mansion just outside Oxted in Surrey, was his primary residence. It's a beautiful Grade I-listed property built in the early 17th century, a sprawling Tudor-style manor with distinctive red-brick construction sitting at the heart of meticulously designed grounds. There's a formal garden adjacent to the house, whose rigorous geometric pattern of quadrants is defined by pale pathways. How impressive it must have looked to those young women, driven down the long road to this classic English country estate.

CARLA

Carla* was interviewed for a position as a governess at Barrow Green Court when she was seventeen. 'I wasn't quite sure what a governess was, but from the job description it looked like a nanny position and I had lots of experience as a nanny, so I went for it. I remember saying at the interview that I was confused by the term "governess", and the woman who was interviewing told me not to worry, and that the house owners had probably been watching *The Sound of Music* or something.

'She said it was a straightforward nannying job but then asked me lots of personal questions. She wanted to know how many boyfriends I'd had, whether I'd had any venereal diseases and whether I'd ever been tested for them. I must have looked shocked, but she reassured me and said that if I hadn't, the family would pay for me to have tests. For some reason this reassured me and I took the job.'

Her first day in the job worked like a dream. She arrived to find her room ready for her. 'I've read reports of people arriving for jobs at the Fayed family home and being shoved in tiny windowless rooms, but that's not my memory of the place. I remember it being the most beautiful house I'd ever seen. My room was quite big, and someone had put some flowers in a vase on the bedside table. The place was heavenly, with beautiful gardens. When I arrived, I was so excited to be there.'

The excitement did not last long. There was a knock on her door early the next morning and she was summoned to meet Fayed. She assumed she would be meeting the children and brought along some toys that she had brought with her. But when she reached Fayed there were no children there.

'He looked at the toys I had with me and told me never to bring anything like that into the house because they might have germs. Then he told me to come and sit on his knee. I walked slowly over to him, and he grabbed me and pulled me onto him. He shoved his hand up my leg and under my skirt and squeezed my breasts. We hadn't spoken more than a handful of words and he was abusing me.'

Carla managed to wriggle free and headed towards the door. 'I stopped and turned to him and said, "Please call me when the children are here and I'll look after them," but he said, "The children won't be here much over the next few days. We have time to get to know one another."' She rushed back to her room and found two men in there installing a telephone. Once they'd left, she picked up the receiver and called her mum.

'I told Mum I'd made a big mistake and wanted to come home. I started to tell her what he'd done, but then the phone cut off. A minute later it rang, and I picked it up, thinking it was mum. It wasn't. It was someone telling me to go and see the boss immediately.'

Carla says she was terrified when she went to see him. He told her that he knew about the call she'd made and she must never tell anyone about what happened in the house. He said that the contract she'd signed meant that she could never speak about anything, and if she did, she'd go to jail. She was also told that she now needed to sign an NDA.

'I didn't know what an NDA was, and I wanted to leave, but he really scared me. Once I'd signed the contract his mood changed considerably and he told me that I should take the day to enjoy myself. He said that someone would come to show me round. He was like that – his mood would shift suddenly. You never knew whether he was going to be really nasty or really nice.'

Carla was taken around the grand house and told that she could use the pool to swim and relax. 'I went into my room to change into my swimming costume, and while I was naked he came in. He pushed me back onto the bed and his hands were all over me. I tried desperately to push him off and shout for help, but it was no good. I was so terrified that I was quite weak, so I lay there crying while he raped me.'

Carla got dressed and ran out of the house. 'I don't know how far I ran and walked for – it was miles. Then a car pulled up and offered to take me to the station. It was someone from Fayed's house. He told me that he would give me some money for the train if I promised never to say anything to anyone. He also reminded me about the form I'd signed. I was petrified into silence.' She never contacted the police.

'Since that day, and particularly since the BBC documentary, I have heard of other women who worked as nannies, chefs, cleaners and housekeepers. All of them were hired as targets for abuse.'

JERRI

At Villa Windsor, the Ritz, on Fayed's private plane and his yacht, women were sexually abused. He took every opportunity. A former BBC make-up artist was sexually assaulted at Villa Windsor while doing the make-up for an episode of *The Clothes Show* based at the mansion in the late 1980s.

On his plane he attacked Jerri MacDonald, a twenty-eight-year-old who moved from Cheshire to south-east England for what she thought was her dream job as a stewardess for Fayair (later called Harrods Aviation). But in her first broadcast interview, she told Sky News how it quickly became a nightmare, and how she felt 'like a deer in headlights' when he insisted she accompany him to the Paris Ritz.

To begin with, she said he wasn't overly forward. He would hug her, kiss her on the cheek and give her money. But on her third trip things were different. 'I remember sitting on a chair and not having any idea that he had appeared behind me. He placed his hand straight into my blouse,' she said. 'Luckily I managed to grab and lift his hand back out.' On another occasion, she said Fayed called her one evening and asked her to come to London on the pretext of doing some 'office work'. She made the journey in from Essex, and after working late she spent the night in one of his suites. 'I noticed there were no locks on the doors at all. So I felt very vulnerable,' she said. 'I was sat on the settee, and then the next minute he let himself in and came over to me. I was kind of startled. And then he just stood there and said, "Stand up, stand up."

'So I stood up and then he just grabbed my hand and said, "Come on, we'll go to the bedroom. We have sex."' She refused, which angered him a great deal. 'He could get very angry,' she says. On one occasion she pushed him away when he tried to kiss her. 'He completely turned on me, just started swearing and just told me, you know, "You're a stupid girl. What did you think I invited you here for? I want to have sex with you. I don't want you to work on my jets any more. You can work in the offices."' Around a week after that incident she received a call to say she was fired.

The pattern of abuse extended beyond British shores, creating a global network of suffering linked by Fayed's business empire. His international properties served as staging grounds for assault, with each venue carefully controlled to facilitate his predation and silence his victims.

There were so many allegations of rape and sexual assaults at the Ritz Hotel that French prosecutors are involved. They're investigating the rapes that took place and the 'cult-like' hotel management that enabled the attacks. There are thought to be twenty claims of rape at the hotel in Paris, but the police say they are talking to many more women, and that number is set to rise significantly. Even Interpol have been involved in trying to establish what happened, when it happened, and who was involved.

KRISTINA

Kristina Svensson was an executive assistant at the Ritz between 1998 and 2000 and claims that a lot of people who worked with her there knew about Fayed's behaviour. She said that women were being trafficked around the world, drugged and attacked. She told the BBC: 'You can put enough fluff around it and whatever you want. But he was hiring vulnerable women and using coercive control – himself and his entourage – to traffic these women. Period. That's it. There's nothing else to be said.'

Svensson recalls an incident when Fayed groped her and 'walked away like giggling or laughing' afterwards. 'I didn't really want to go close to him because I was afraid he would do it again.' She said that during her time at the Ritz in Paris, he asked her to come to London, where he said she would be his 'girlfriend'.

Her tactic, to stop him groping her, was to hold something against her chest – a book or handbag. 'He would put his hand up my skirt as I was trying to get out of the chair and the whole time I'm thinking, I'm a professional.

I'm a professional. He's going to realise this and this is going to stop. It's going to end at some point.'

In a statement, the Ritz Paris said:

> We are deeply troubled by the recent testimonies regarding the late Mohamed Al Fayed. The Ritz Paris does not tolerate any form of violence or sexual coercion and would like to express its deepest sympathy to the women who have come forward. The hotel upholds the highest standards of professionalism and has a steadfast commitment to fostering an environment where employees and guests are treated with respect and integrity. The safety and well-being of our employees and guests is our absolute priority. We are determined to shed light on these allegations, in line with our commitment to transparency towards our guests and employees.

The timeline of abuse spanning nearly five decades suggests a pattern of behaviour so entrenched, so methodical, that it defined his entire adult life. His businesses, his properties, his philanthropic endeavours – all served as elaborate facades behind which a serial predator operated with impunity.

The stories from Fulham FC to the Ritz, from his private plane to his country estate, paint a picture not of isolated incidents but of a carefully constructed empire of abuse. Each venue represented another opportunity, each business acquisition another hunting ground. The true cost of Fayed's business empire should not be calculated in pounds or dollars, but in the shattered lives he left in his wake.

At least he was never awarded British citizenship. Fayed paid MPs to ask questions in Parliament on his behalf in order to highlight his plight. It made no difference. So, he hit the nuclear button and told the world that he had paid cash to two Conservative ministers, Neil Hamilton and Tim Smith, to ask questions.

The scandal deepened when Fayed revealed that Jonathan Aitken, then a cabinet minister, had been staying for free at the Ritz in Paris at the same time as a group of Saudi arms dealers. Aitken would eventually serve time in prison for lying about the affair in court. Fayed's vendetta against the Conservative Party inflicted lasting damage, contributing to public perceptions of 'Tory sleaze' that helped end eighteen years of Conservative rule and usher in the era of New Labour. But all of this did nothing to change the government's position on Mohamed Fayed. His brother, Ali, was granted British citizenship in 1999, but Mohamed's application was rejected. Jack Straw, the Home Secretary, later described Fayed as a bully 'used to getting his own way'.

For a man whose entire life had been dedicated to transcending his origins and reinventing himself, it was the ultimate reminder that some barriers cannot be overcome with money, power or fabricated credentials.

12

'I ONLY LASTED A DAY'

ONE WOMAN'S VIEW FROM
THE DESIGNER DEPARTMENT

'I don't like fat people. You are perfect
– slim and tall.'

Fayed to Amelia, shortly before attacking her

AMELIA

Amelia floats into the room like she's walking on set to star in a shampoo advert. She's pencil slim, with silky blonde hair that settles into waves around her shoulders. She takes a seat, crosses her unfeasibly long legs at the ankle and adjusts the expensive cashmere wrap over her tiny shoulders. She was born in Sweden and has classic Swedish colouring: peaches and cream skin, blue eyes and gleaming white teeth. One can only imagine how beautiful she was when she arrived in London twenty years ago as an eighteen-year-old.

'My family moved to England for my father's job in banking,' she says. 'He was a businessman, and an opportunity came up here. At the time I didn't know what I was going to do with my life . . . I'd been a pole-vaulter when I was younger and I thought I'd have a future in that, maybe go to the Olympics, but I was quite badly injured so had to retire early. It was a difficult time. But London sounded fun.'

Amelia was walking into Wimbledon Village a few days after arriving when she was stopped by a man who ran a modelling agency. He pushed a business card into her hand, telling her to have a think about it and call him.

'I ended up modelling for a catalogue – mainly shoes – so you couldn't even see what I looked like in most of the pictures, but it went well, and I was asked to go to a casting for a TV advert. Unfortunately, I didn't get the advert but another girl at the agency did, and she told me about a small recruitment agency near Sloane Square station in Chelsea where they found jobs for models and actresses who were between jobs. "You can just drop the job when any modelling work comes up," she told me.'

This agency has been mentioned a number of times in my research, but no details about it seem to be available. Amelia says it only placed people at Harrods and always put female applicants on the beauty floor.

'The woman at the agency said that's all they do – just recruit out-of-work models and actors. It sounded quite odd, but I liked the idea of working for Harrods so I went ahead and found myself with a job.'

The agency had recruited a man to work as a fashion supervisor in a new high-end men's fashion concession that was just opening, and Amelia to work on the beauty floor, but when she arrived for her first day, the male model had been offered a job the previous day so he'd pulled out, and Amelia was told to go to menswear instead.

Amelia was taken through to an induction, during which it became clear that the staff thought she had a lot of retail management experience. 'I had none. I'd been an athlete. I once worked in a chemist's shop in Sweden, but not in management. The agency seemed to have told them that I was experienced and should be fast-tracked into senior management. I decided to go with it. I didn't expect to be there that long.'

Amelia was told that style, deportment and a smile were vitally important, as she and her staff were the faces of the brand. She had staff working under her, and it would be her job to make sure they understood their responsibilities. She was told that she needed to watch the staff carefully and report anything untoward. 'They seemed very keen to emphasise that my role was as a policeman in the department. They didn't mention anything about making the staff feel needed, confident or important. It was all about snooping around and making sure that no one was doing anything wrong.'

She had to compile notes through the week to show how hard people were working, keeping information about their hours, their dress, their engagement with customers and various other things. 'It all felt very odd . . . like they were saying, "Try and catch them out," as if the more negatives I could list, the better supervisor I was.'

Amelia was in situ, helping customers and making sure the shelves were properly stocked, when Fayed and a woman approached her.

'The woman was incredibly attractive, very glamorous and well put-together with a mane of perfectly styled blonde hair. She was the sort of woman you yearn to look like.'

Fayed walked over and said he was very glad that she'd come to work at Harrods. 'He said he thought I'd fit in well and he saw a bright future for me. I thanked him, but because I didn't plan to stay at Harrods long, I wasn't terribly bothered. After he'd gone, a woman came up and asked me what my name was. I told her, and she said that the chairman really liked me, and it would be worth me playing along with him and doing what he wanted. I'd be rewarded if I did.

'She told me that she had started working for Fayed in a menswear concession and been promoted, so that she was now in a senior position. She said it as if to imply that I too could rise through the ranks, if I just did as I was asked.'

The woman was Kelly Walker-Duncalf. Around half an hour after she left, Amelia was told by a floor supervisor that she needed to go up to Fayed's office.

'I was escorted there. The whole experience was baffling.'

She was taken to his office, and when she walked in she saw a gas mask on the side and asked him what it was for. He explained that he wore it when he travelled by helicopter from his Surrey home to London because he didn't want to inhale fumes. He then gave her a short lecture on how much he hated germs.

He asked her to come and sit next to him and told her she was beautiful. Then he put his hand on her thigh and commented on how long and slim her legs were. 'I don't like fat people. You are perfect – slim and tall,' he said. 'Short people are not beautiful.' Then he asked her whether she had a boyfriend.

'I said that I didn't and asked him why he was asking that. I started to get dirty old man vibes from him, so I pulled my chair away from his. He looked horrified and told me to bring my chair back or I'd make him unhappy. He said I was feisty and he liked that, but he needed me to be sitting right next to him so he could talk to me properly.

'Probably because I'm from Sweden and not English, I'm less worried about offending people, so I told him I wanted to leave and stood up. He immediately stood up as well and grabbed me, pulling at my blouse and fondling my breasts, so I pushed him hard, and he went staggering backwards. He shouted loudly, presumably in Egyptian, and two men burst in through the door.'

Amelia says that when they saw him on the floor, they ran over to tend to him as if he were a small child who'd just fallen off a swing, asking whether he needed an ambulance. Amelia ran back down to the sales floor and told the team there what had happened. They were open-mouthed.

'They seemed more worried about the fact that I pushed the chairman than they did about the fact that he sexually abused me.

'Of course I pushed him. I'm not an idiot. I'm not going to stand there and take it.'

She says that as soon as she saw their reaction, she knew she'd be sacked.

'To be honest, I didn't care. Who wants to work there, for a guy like that? I don't want to be cruel, but all these women who stayed working for him when they knew what he was like . . . what were they thinking? What was wrong with them?

'You can't work for someone like that. You have to have more respect for yourself. I gave him a shove and left. I then left the store, went back to the recruitment agency and told them what happened. They phoned the store to tell them I wouldn't be coming back.

'I realise that it was easier for me because the job didn't matter as much as it did for other people – it was just a stop gap.'

If the job had been something she desperately needed to keep hold of, how much more vulnerable would she have been, and how much worse could the outcome have been as a result?

Amelia went for a drink that evening with a woman called Louise who worked at the agency, as well as a couple of models who'd also worked at Harrods through the agency.

'One of the women had been asked to leave because Mohamed saw her smoking outside the building on one of the security cameras. He said he couldn't stand smoking and wouldn't employ anyone who smoked. When she said she wasn't on company property and was free to do whatever she liked out of work as long as it was legal, he got very angry and said she could no longer work for him.

'I heard a great deal about the role that Kelly Walker-Duncalf played, and how she rang up the agency frequently, asking them to send attractive women who could be a "chairman's girl". I didn't think about it all too deeply at the time but I guess they meant that they wanted her to send women for him to abuse.

'They told me lots of amusing things about Mohamed's mad spending sprees. He bought several of Liberace's pianos, apparently, and a painting titled *Harrods on Waikiki Beach* [by the actor Tony Curtis].

'They talked about Salah Fayed, the "third brother", who was nicknamed "Fruit Bat" because he only came out at night. Apparently, he once bought two eighteen-inch miniature horses that he would walk up and down Park Lane on a lead until Mohamed took them off him.'

Louise told Amelia how sorry she was about what had happened. She said they knew he was a handful, but had absolutely no idea that he would ever physically attack anyone. Louise said that she knew he liked pretty girls working there, and particularly those who were well educated and had white skin, but she'd never heard of anyone being attacked by him before and urged Amelia to go to the police. She said she would, but never did.

'Louise said there used to be a section on the application form for Harrods that asked for a person's colour, race, ethnic background, etc. The form also asked for height, weight and waist measurements. When the agency challenged the questions and said it was illegal to ask for personal information like that on an application form, Walker-Duncalf said that, in that case, every application had to be submitted with a photograph.'

Amelia then sent a letter to Harrods, on the instruction of her father, who found the reports of his behaviour far more troubling than Amelia had.

'I suppose, looking back, I didn't care that much, but my dad was furious and he looked up to see who the CEO was in order to contact him and make a complaint about the chairman. It took him a while to work out who it was, because of the fast turnover of staff. Senior managers were being sacked so frequently that it was impossible to work out who was there, and who had gone. In the end, I managed to persuade him not to make a formal complaint. I do remember how appalled he was at the whole set-up there, though, with all these senior executives coming and going.'

Her father was right: the turnover of CEOs took place with incredible speed. Jon Brilliant, a former CEO, was at Harrods for eighteen months (he said that to work there any longer than that you'd need to have a 'frontal lobotomy'), and Max Rigelman lasted just two months.

Most told Fayed they were leaving because he was too interfering and it was impossible to get anything done. Fayed would counter by saying that he was willing to pay money and he expected his demands to be met. By 'pay money' he meant hand over an envelope stuffed with notes

– that was his way of working. Brilliant estimates that he received £50,000 in brown envelopes, but even that wasn't enough to persuade him to stay in a 'nasty, toxic environment'.

Amelia's father, himself a high-flying businessman at a London bank, made further investigations into Fayed and his conduct. His enquiries made him keenly aware of the racism, snobbism and sexism that pervaded the store, and these troubled him. It seemed as if everything Fayed wanted was just for his own private purposes, not the business. His vision for Harrods was to fill it with lots of beautiful girls, then sleep with them.

'One thing I realised from all the conversations with the models at the agency,' says Amelia, 'and from what my dad said, is that lots of people knew what was going on. How could they not?

'I sent a letter in to Harrods HR department, which detailed my anger at what had happened. I received a response from a guy there, so we can be sure that he knew what was going on. The secretary who typed out the letter knew, some of the security guys knew. I mean, in my incident alone, I reckon about ten people could have known.

13

DECADES APART

THE ABUSE OVER FOUR DECADES

'This was a seriously bad man. I can give you
examples of people just disappearing.'

Penny, who worked for Fayed in the 1980s

The predator did not emerge fully formed. Like any skilled hunter, Fayed's methods of exploitation evolved over time, becoming more refined and systematic. What began as opportunistic encounters in the 1980s transformed into a calculated enterprise of abuse spanning four decades, protected by wealth, power and a carefully constructed shield of enablers.

This chapter traces the chilling progression of Fayed's predatory behaviour through the testimony of four women, each representing a different decade of his reign of terror. Through their stories, separated by years but united by similar horrors, a pattern emerges of a man who didn't simply abuse power, but perfected its misuse over time.

The journey begins in the 1980s with Penny Simpson, whose experience as one of Fayed's personal assistants reveals his early patterns of intimidation and control. Moving into the 1990s, Jenny's story illustrates how Fayed's methods became more brazen as his confidence grew. By the 2000s, as Bianca Gascoigne's account shows, his predatory behaviour extended to targeting much younger women, grooming them with the promise of career advancement. Finally, Yvonne's harrowing experience in 2010 demonstrates the sophisticated operation Fayed had developed by his later years, complete with the recruiters and enablers who facilitated his crimes.

PENNY

Penny Simpson worked for Fayed in the 1980s. She was a PA and an air hostess, and never felt comfortable in his company.

'He's very sinister, and this isn't just hindsight,' she told the *Daily Telegraph*. 'You were very aware that he was a scary and quite formidable personality. He surrounded himself with the trappings of security guards and doormen. He never liked moving anywhere without a posse.

'This was a seriously bad man. I can give you examples of people just disappearing. I knew the security people he worked with, and I just knew that something bad would happen to me. He had a long reach, and I suspect that not a tenth of it has come out.'

When Penny applied to work for Harrods, she was interviewed by Fayed himself. She remembers him telling her that no one who worked for him had ever had to sign an NDA. This is odd on a number of fronts, first because he categorically did make people sign NDAs, all the time.

Those who didn't sign them were made well aware that if they said anything, they or their family would be harmed. 'He had some seriously nasty friends,' Penny recalls. 'And the climate was very different back then. A woman alleging sexual assault would not have been believed.'

Penny remembers the extravagant store walks during which he looked for women, and the way he was accompanied everywhere by a large posse.

From her two years there, Penny says what she remembers most is 'the constant battle we waged against germs. The incessant washing and drying of crockery and glasses with tissues. We travelled with crates of Kleenex and wet wipes with which we'd swab door handles and lavatory levers and lift buttons. Room service was always re-plated on dishes we had personally sanitised, and table tops and chair arms disinfected after each guest departed. Fayed had doctors ready to test prospective victims for sexual and other diseases.'

She was well aware of his voracious sexual appetite. She says that Friday nights were always 'play nights', and Fayed would receive a call from a woman who'd arrange to drop a young girl off for him to 'play with'. It was seedy, but at least these women came willingly, knowing what they were getting involved in.

Penny says that, as well as being a womaniser, Fayed loved wealth and fame, and he relished the opportunity to entertain stars at his Park Lane apartments. 'In quiet periods,' she recalls, 'my job was compiling a Rolodex the size of a small Ferris wheel. Many different hands had filled out its thousands of index cards. Mohamed would deposit scraps of paper on my desk with scrawled titbits; "younger wife" or "vintage Patek Philippe".'

Although Fayed tried it on with Penny a few times, she told him she wasn't interested and managed to keep him at arms' length.

JENNY

A former ballet dancer and beauty queen, Jenny was used to getting attention, but not usually in the gym changing room. In 1991, she was showering after a particularly arduous training session when the woman changing next to her commented how much she liked Jenny's boots. 'Then, as I went to leave the changing room,' says Jenny, 'the woman came running after me and said I should come and work at Harrods. She introduced herself as "Mohamed Al-Fayed's right-hand woman".'

Jenny was flattered, and as she'd always wanted to work in fashion, she gave the woman her number. By the time she got home there was a message for her, inviting her to the store the next day. 'I couldn't believe how quick it all was. Also, I couldn't understand why she was keen on me – I was just a random woman in the gym who had nice boots on. They were acting as if I was some sort of fashion aficionado.'

When she entered the Harrods building she was taken straight to Fayed's office to meet the boss. 'He asked me what department I'd like to work in. It was the oddest meeting. He held my hand and told me I could make a lot of money and be very successful at Harrods. It was surreal. Why would a billionaire, a famous man, care about a random shop assistant?'

She decided to put his attentions down to kindness and the desire to foster a good working relationship with all staff, regardless of their level in the company. So she took the job, and for eighteen months she worked as one of Fayed's PAs.

'It was awful. Just the most terrifying and demeaning time of my life. One of his other secretaries would call for me to come into his office, and I'd try anything not to go . . . I'd say I felt sick, or needed to go to the toilet, or anything, but it always had to be me, and the message would come back to me: "Go and see him now."'

When she went into meetings with him, she was groped, asked for sex and threatened with the loss of her job if she didn't dump her boyfriend. 'I got home from work one night and bawled my eyes out to my boyfriend. He said I had to leave, so the next day I handed in my notice. The boss called me into his office and went nuts. He told me he'd make sure I never got a decent job ever again. I ran towards the door, in tears, but the door was locked. I remember banging on it. Someone would definitely have been able to hear me, but no one came.'

Jenny says that Fayed found this hysterically funny, shouting 'Cry like a baby' at her. Then he told her he'd only open the door if she kissed him. 'I was in this awful

Catch-22 situation. Kiss him and get out of there, or continue to fight him, knowing it would all get nastier.' So she walked back over to him and kissed him while he roughly groped her breasts. 'Then he let me out.'

She sued him for sexual harassment and received a £5,000 settlement if she signed an NDA. 'I had never heard of a non-disclosure agreement before. When I realised what it was, I didn't want to sign it because I didn't want to have to keep silent about what he'd done, but if I didn't sign it, the security guys said he'd make sure I never worked again.

'He was always full of threats to get his own way, putting you into difficult situations where there was no outcome that suited you.

'I wasn't unique in this respect, someone told me about a girl whose dad was a major supplier of washing machines. When she refused to have sex with him, he told her, "I'll make it really hard for your dad to work in this town if you leave this room without having sex with me." When the girl challenged him, he said, "Your father will die a pauper." She slept with him because she was so worried about what would happen to her dad. When the sex was over, she was sacked, and he cancelled her father's contract to supply washing machines to Harrods.'

Jenny was asked to participate in the BBC documentary but was reluctant to talk so publicly about what happened to her. 'When I saw how good the documentary was, and how much power there was in all these women speaking out, I realised that I was wrong, and I should have done it to help others, but when they asked me, it felt like it would all be too traumatic.'

When Jenny left Harrods, she went to work at Selfridges. 'Several of us who were sacked from Harrods, applied for jobs there because it was nearby and very similar work. It seemed like an obvious place to apply.'

Emma worked at Selfridges in the early to mid-1990s and remembers seeing the state that the Harrods girls were in when they arrived. 'They'd be terrified every time a senior manager came onto the floor. So many times, I found myself saying, "It's not like that here . . . they won't attack you." Fancy having to say that to an employee. These women had got so used to expecting awful things to happen to them that they couldn't imagine anything different.

'For a lot of them, it was their first job, and I suppose they didn't know anything about the world of work and blamed themselves for what happened to them. No matter how many times I said "It's not like Harrods here," you'd see the alarm on their face if a manager walked onto the sales floor.'

BIANCA

Bianca Gascoigne was just sixteen when she went to work at Harrods in 2004. She was very familiar with the store, having visited with her parents – England footballing hero Paul Gascoigne (she's his adopted daughter) and her mum

Sheryl. She recalls going to Harrods for lunch, and every time they walked in, Fayed would come bounding over. He was very personable, very charming and very welcoming, bringing gifts with him and always stopping to talk to her. She felt very safe around him. He knew her parents, he was a nice guy.

When she left school, Bianca was very clear that she wanted to become a fashion buyer. She knew Harrods and loved the place, and her parents were friends with the guy who owned it, so it seemed like the perfect place to go to try and kick off her career. She started work there as a temp, spending time working across lots of different departments, then she settled in one place – on the ladies' fashion floor. From there, she worked her way up to become a fashion buyer, based in the office.

Her new role meant she would have to deal with Fayed a lot more. This didn't strike her as a problem; she'd known him for years. She'd have to talk to him about key decisions she was making and take reports to him on a weekly basis. This is when the grooming started. It was words of flattery at first – he told her he'd always be there for her and that she was doing a good job. Once he had flattered her into trusting him, he began to make her feel unstable by bringing up her dad's alcoholism and did all he could to make her feel vulnerable about her home life. He told her that he would be a father figure to her.

Things then progressed into physical affection. She recalls him touching her and leaning over to kiss her. The gentle kisses on the lips turned into more aggressive actions, as he tried to force his tongue down her throat. 'How I dealt with it was pretty much an out-of-body experience,' she says, 'like I was looking down on what was going on, but not really registering what was *actually* going on with me at the time because I was super-scared.'

She never told anyone about this and says she felt ashamed. 'I felt dirty, I felt I just pretended like it wasn't happening. I put it in a box and moved on and was trying to deal with it. I couldn't even bring myself to mention it to anyone. I've only just told my mum recently exactly what went down, because I just didn't want to upset any of the family.

'And it's just bizarre why you shut down in that moment when really, we should have a voice and we should speak up.'

So Bianca kept quiet, and Fayed kept pushing. She was due to fly to Milan on a buying job, which, for a sixteen-year-old, was an incredible thrill. Fayed had invited her to spend the night in his apartment so she didn't have to go home that evening and could get to the airport quickly in the morning.

What she didn't expect was that Fayed would show up at the flat. 'I didn't expect him in any shape or form to turn up,' she says. 'I was completely shocked and gobsmacked, and didn't know what to do. You know . . . I'm in his apartment. What do I do? I thought, no, you're not coming in. But obviously, he came in. It was his place. And that's obviously the worst ordeal that I had to go through, and that's what I've been dealing with for a very long time.'

Fayed attempted to force himself onto her. He grabbed her hand and tried to place it in his groin, he undid his trousers and tried to force her to touch his penis, and he pushed her head down onto his penis. Bianca says she wriggled out of the situation. 'It's all a bit of a blur, to be honest, because it's something that I've really tried to block out.'

She says there had been warning signs, but she didn't act. She recalls a time, soon after she started working at the store, when he offered to buy her an apartment. Her mum went in to meet Fayed to discuss it and immediately said, 'This is a red flag.'

Bianca wishes she'd said something then and told her mother how uncomfortable he made her feel. 'That was a chance to tell her, but I didn't because I was so scared, and he was such a powerful man.'

When she first spoke publicly about her experiences with Fayed, soon after the BBC documentary aired, she received numerous messages from women telling her about their encounters with him. She finds it upsetting that so many women went through the same thing and that their stories were brushed under the carpet, meaning he got away with this behaviour for decades.

'I think it was pretty much a common-knowledge thing that it was going on. So it makes me upset to think of my sixteen-year-old self suffering like that. It makes me sad that I didn't go and talk to people in the office. Then we'd have worked out how bad it was and maybe done something.'

After her experiences at Harrods, Bianca began drinking heavily to cope. 'I just wanted to numb out a lot of the emotions that I was feeling.' Now she's coping without resorting to alcohol, and has found talking about what happened to be hugely helpful.

'Because of the number of messages that I've had, I don't feel so isolated any more. I don't feel alone. Since I've shared my news, the healing that I've done, it's been very empowering. And I really would love to encourage anyone that's been through anything, just to speak to a friend.

'Hopefully, in future, especially for my daughter's generation, big companies will focus on these things that can go down when someone so powerful is in charge, and they won't be able to get away with it. I hope more women come forward and find their voice and know that it's not just them. They're not alone.'

YVONNE

In January 2010, at the age of twenty, Yvonne was introduced to Kelly Walker-Duncalf by a mutual friend. 'She was this incredibly glamorous woman who was high up in this amazing store, and I was flattered to be introduced to her, to be honest. We chatted and she was really friendly. I kept thinking, *Why does someone like that want to be friends with someone like me?* She was so put-together and beautifully dressed, I was totally in awe and enjoyed spending time with her. Then one day, she told me that Mohamed Fayed was looking for three new personal assistants and was I interested? One of the new employees would be based in Paris. It all sounded too good to be true so I told her I'd love to be considered for it.'

Yvonne was taken to Fayed's Park Lane residence to meet him. 'I thought he was lovely. Very friendly and encouraging, and he said how he could help my career. He told me it was a good place to work and there was always lots of money for people who worked hard.'

When they left, Fayed handed an envelope full of cash to Walker-Duncalf and offered the same to Yvonne.

'I didn't know what to do. Was this for wages? Or was I being paid to attend the interview? None of it made any sense. So I turned to Kelly and whispered, "What's it for?" She said, "It's for you. Shall I carry it for you?"'

Walker-Duncalf led Yvonne back to the lifts, explaining that Fayed was very generous and did that for people all the time. When they got to the ground floor, she insisted that they go out for the evening. They went to a bar and Walker-Duncalf bought champagne, but Yvonne started to feel unwell after just a glass.

'Everything was a bit blurry after that, but I think Kelly took a call – or pretended to take a call – from Fayed, and said that he'd offered me a job and would like to see me again to talk about it. I felt very wobbly and unsure of myself. Kelly said she'd get me a glass of water and handed it to me and told me to drink it all down, but when I drank it, it was champagne. I was starting to feel really ill.'

Yvonne doesn't remember going into Fayed's room, but she remembers being there, and Fayed tugging at her clothes to get them off. She was wearing a body under her suit (a garment much like a swimming costume), and Fayed couldn't work out how to remove it.

'I have this memory of him pushing and pulling and swearing and shouting, "Take it off," but I couldn't have done so even if I'd wanted to. I was incapable of doing anything. After groping me and fighting with my clothes for what felt like hours, he gave up and told me to get dressed.

'I couldn't get my clothes on, I was all over the place, my head was spinning, my legs had turned to jelly. I was scared, you know? Really scared. I didn't understand what was happening to me. I staggered out of the apartment and fell onto the floor. Someone helped me to put my clothes on. It was a woman, but not Kelly. I've no idea who she was. I'm so grateful I was wearing the bodysuit.'

Yvonne got herself home that evening, but has no idea how she did it. She woke up late the next day to a message from Walker-Duncalf. 'Hope you enjoyed your evening. Let's catch up soon.'

14

RETRIBUTION

WHEN FAYED WAS CROSSED

'Your shoes are too high – on the floor,
crawl around like a donkey.'

Fayed to an assistant who was wearing flat shoes

Power was not merely about wealth or sexual conquest for Fayed, it was about absolute dominance. As his years at Harrods went by, his confidence grew, and with it, his methods of control expanded beyond the sexual abuse documented in previous chapters. What emerged was a more complex and insidious portrait of a man for whom humiliation became both sport and weapon.

While much of the debate and analysis of Fayed has focused on his sexual predation, following the BBC documentary, the full spectrum of his tyranny extended further. The stories we've told reveal a man whose need for control manifested in increasingly theatrical displays of cruelty – forcing employees to act like animals, fabricating criminal charges against those who dared leave his employ, threatening those who rejected his advances, and systematically breaking down the dignity of anyone who challenged his authority.

Fayed's retribution against those who 'crossed' him illustrates how his abuse evolved over time. No longer content with private acts of violation, he developed a taste for public spectacle, using humiliation to punish the immediate target and warn others not to step out of line. These public displays showed he answered to no moral, ethical or legal standard but his own.

What emerges from these accounts is the profile of a man who derived genuine pleasure from causing distress. For Fayed, his ability to reduce a successful executive to crawling on the floor like a donkey, to strip a valued employee of their livelihood over a perceived slight or to pursue years'-long vendettas against former staff members wasn't merely about maintaining control – it was about feeding a psychological need to see others diminished.

The stories that follow paint a picture not just of a sexual predator, but of a man who built an empire on fear.

PHILIPPA

You hear a surprising amount about donkeys when researching Fayed. The man seems to have been obsessed by them. Politicians were donkeys, his workforce were donkeys and he was the lion who led them. Everyone who ever crossed him was a donkey. It was the ultimate put-down.

Philippa was eighteen when she went to work for Fayed as a PA. On her second day in the job she was called in to a meeting with her new boss and six of her fellow PAs, all older and more experienced than her. When Philippa entered the room she was told to take a seat next to the chairman. The other six PAs were lined up in front of them.

'When I walked in it was clear that he was unhappy about something,' she recalls, 'and this was his way of getting petty revenge. I didn't know why I'd been called in, but I was new to the job so I didn't feel I could ask.'

While Philippa sat there silently, Fayed pointed to the PA at the end of the line and said, 'Your shoes are too high – on the floor, crawl around like a donkey.'

Philippa remembers looking down and seeing the woman had flat shoes on. But that was irrelevant. Fayed wanted to abuse someone, so he'd make up any old reason to do so.

'Like a donkey,' Fayed repeated. 'Quickly. On the floor now.'

Such was the astonishing control that Fayed had over his staff that the woman dropped down onto all fours and started shuffling around the room, braying like a donkey.

'Fayed shouted, "Louder, more like a donkey, bray like a donkey." The woman was crying, which made Fayed laugh. It was horrible and humiliating. Some of the other women who were standing there started crying too and that made him laugh even more.

'Then he said, "Kick, kick" and urged the woman to kick the other women. "Kick more, kick harder. Come on, donkey." Then he threw loads of £20 notes at the woman and told her to pick them up in her mouth. While the woman kicked out, brayed and picked up the notes, Fayed laughed like he'd never seen anything so funny and shouted, "Donkey, donkey." It was awful. Absolutely awful.

'She wasn't allowed to stop until she'd picked up all the money in her mouth, then he said she could stand up. He turned to me and said, "Which one next?", pointing to the line of women. I didn't say anything, and he told me that if I didn't choose one I'd be sacked.

'I think there must have been a knock at the door or a phone rang or something, because he was distracted and dismissed us all.'

Fayed was a man with a need to bring others down in any way he could, and in so doing assert his own power. He liked to dominate, and he liked others to feel and look subservient. He appeared to possess none of the normal human need to make others feel better and valued in his company, indeed quite the opposite. He was at his happiest when making others unhappy.

On one store walk, Fayed was strolling through the store with his entourage, including Ellen* from his private office, when he spotted a man on crutches.

'Find out who that man is,' he said.

Ellen approached the man. 'He told me his name and explained that he'd broken two toes the night before playing football in the Harrods team. I told him he'd done well to come in the next day and asked him whether his foot hurt. He said that it was very painful and his foot was all swollen, but he didn't want to leave the department short-staffed. I thought that was incredible of him. Standing all day with two broken toes would be so painful.

'I went back over to tell Fayed. I thought he'd be thrilled with the man's loyalty, but he didn't want to hear anything. He said, "I don't like cripples – get rid of him."

'I said, "What? Sack him?"

'Fayed looked at me and said, "Yes – no cripples and no fatties. He can leave straight away."'

Richard Coles, the writer, vicar and former member of pop duo the Communards, has an interesting tale that displays Fayed's sense of humour in all its puerile vulgarity: 'I knew a chap who was a foreign diplomat, and when he was posted to London he was invited to lunch by Mohamed Fayed. This seemed a bit peculiar, as if he were expected to present his credentials at Harrods as well as the Court of St James's, but he went. He was shown into the chairman's dining room by a white-gloved butler and there was Fayed, who greeted him fulsomely and said, "Your Excellency, I have a gift for you! Hold out your hand!"

'He held out his hand.

'"And close your eyes!"

'He closed his eyes and something was laid on his palm.

'"Open your eyes!"

'It was a strip of Viagra.'

CHRISTOPH

Christoph Bettermann saw a less 'hilarious' side to Fayed. He worked as the deputy chairman of Harrods and chairman of Harrods Estates. He was hugely successful and much admired by Fayed. In 1991 he resigned and told Fayed the good news that he was going to marry Francesca Armitage, a solicitor in the legal department.

Fayed was furious. When valued members of staff left, he saw it as a huge betrayal. He wanted revenge. This started with him being incredibly rude about Armitage and offering to show Bettermann the reports of two gynaecological examinations that had been performed on Armitage, entirely unnecessarily. He also told Bettermann that he'd tried to get Armitage to have sex with him when they were on a trip to Paris. Not satisfied with humiliating Bettermann's future wife in this way, he banned all employees of Harrods from attending the couple's wedding and said those who went would be instantly dismissed.

His actions were staggeringly vindictive, and clearly played fast and loose with the fundamentals of employment law. But that was just the start. Next, he invented a story that Bettermann had stolen $900,000 from him. The false accusations led to Bettermann facing civil and criminal proceedings in Dubai, where the alleged fraud had supposedly taken place.

This caused Bettermann a huge amount of grief – his passport was taken off him and he was summoned to court twenty-five times over the next two years. The charges were dismissed in the end, of course, because they were entirely trumped up. Bettermann was paid almost £300,000, then he sued Fayed for libel in the British courts and won a further £125,000 libel damages, plus £287,500 costs. In total, it's estimated that the whole performance cost Fayed over £1 million. And what for? Because making people feel bad made Fayed feel good.

Graham Jones, the Harrods financial director for three years, found himself in a similarly absurd position. He tendered his resignation and Fayed turned on him. Again, revenge took the form of an accusation of fraud. Jones headed for Australia to visit family in Sydney, but while his plane was still on the tarmac at Heathrow, the police boarded it and arrested him. The reason for the arrest was that Macnamara had falsely claimed that Jones was leaving the country to escape the charges.

Jones was interviewed by police – while Macnamara listened in – and was released in time to catch another plane to Australia later that day. But Fayed had not quite finished with his former director of finance.

When Jones was appointed finance director at Qantas, Fayed set up briefings to inform all the press that Jones was facing a fraud probe and was an unsuitable person to be working at the airline. His new company investigated fully and concluded there was no case to answer.

'Fayed did not take rejection well,' says Susan Long, with considerable understatement. She worked in the Harrods office in the early years of Fayed's reign. 'I was an older woman, so I was never hassled by him and I think he only kept me there to make sure that work was done. I should point out that there were only a couple of us doing all the work. Heaven knows if I hadn't been there, nothing would have happened in that office. There were all these beautiful women milling around, he'd brought them up from the sales floor and they had no admin experience and no guidance . . . they weren't sure what job they were supposed to be doing, so they just sat there.'

Susan says she was reasonably aware of what was happening behind the locked doors of Fayed's office. 'Not rape. I didn't know about anyone being raped or attacked or anything – definitely not – but I realised he had beautiful women in the office, you'd have been blind not to, and I knew he'd call them in to see him, and they'd come out clutching fistfuls of money. So I guessed what was going on.

'You'd see them arriving in expensive jewellery and with handbags that cost more than they made in a year. He'd call them in and want to grope or fondle them. If they said "no" after he'd given them a load of jewellery and money, he'd be furious. I know this doesn't sound very feminist of me, but I saw his point of view. Some of those women needed to be more savvy. I'd want to scream, "Don't take the handbags and the jewellery or he'll think you owe him something."

'I used to think the women were silly for doing it. You can't take money off someone like him and not expect that he wants something for it. Why is he going to give you a £15,000 handbag? For God's sake, he's a man driven by power. He wants something from you.'

When I stop Susan to remind her that women were treated brutally inside his office, many of them never recovering from what he put them through, and – handbag or no handbag – he behaved appallingly, she softens a little.

'I know. It's terrible. Everything about the stories I've heard is appalling, and if I'd known I would have said something, or offered support. But I do wish these women had been a bit more wide-eyed about what was going on and done something to save themselves. He was furious when he was angered . . . I've never known anything like it before or since. Why would you take something from a man like that? He'd think that was a huge rejection. Don't take a £10k bag off a man. Don't do it.'

She says that Fayed was at his all-time worst when he suffered rejection. He couldn't abide it in any way. 'Even being told that products hadn't arrived yet, or that a perfume wasn't selling as well as he wanted it to – he'd be furious and someone was always to blame. He took everything personally and had a huge ego and huge pride.'

This inability to tolerate rejection defined much of Fayed's reign at Harrods. It wasn't simply an unpleasant personality quirk but the driving force behind his most destructive behaviours. For a man who demanded absolute control, any form of rejection – whether a woman declining his advances, an employee resigning or even a supplier failing to deliver – represented a challenge to his self-image as all-powerful.

What might appear as petty tyranny to outsiders was in fact something far more dangerous: a man who viewed other people's autonomy as a personal affront. This explains why his retribution was always disproportionate to the perceived slight. When someone said 'no' to Fayed, they weren't simply declining a request; they were, in his distorted worldview, attacking the very foundation of his identity. And for that, no punishment was too severe, no vendetta too prolonged, no humiliation too extreme.

15

THE ENABLERS' NETWORK

WHY DIDN'T THEY SAY ANYTHING?

'Kelly told me I was ridiculous, and I should have let him do whatever he wanted. He was the richest man in the world, women everywhere wanted to sleep with him.'

Jess, a victim of Fayed, on
Kelly Walker-Duncalf's advice to her

No predator of Fayed's magnitude could operate without a carefully cultivated network of enablers. What began as isolated incidents of misconduct gradually evolved into a sophisticated system of exploitation, supported by an expanding web of complicit individuals across all levels of the Harrods hierarchy. As Fayed's power and confidence grew, so did the complexity and reach of the network that facilitated his crimes.

In the beginning, Fayed's inappropriate behaviour – the personal assistant asked to schedule an unusual private meeting, the bodyguard instructed to ensure certain areas remained undisturbed – might have been dismissed as the eccentricities of a powerful businessman. Nothing here stood out as too odd. But these minor requests established a foundation of unquestioning compliance. Those who followed orders were rewarded generously; those who questioned them quickly found themselves ostracised or dismissed.

As time passed, Fayed's demands grew bolder, his criminal activities more brazen. What started as inappropriate comments or uncomfortable encounters escalated to sexual assault. Alongside this escalation, the network of enablers expanded and became more organised. No longer were these isolated individuals following questionable orders – they became active participants in identifying potential victims, creating opportunities for abuse, and ensuring Fayed's actions remained hidden from public scrutiny.

The most disturbing aspect of this evolution was how ordinary people became accomplices. From technical staff who maintained surveillance systems to human resources personnel who processed complaints without action, from department managers who identified attractive staff to recruiters who specifically targeted young women – each played their part in a system that served Fayed's predatory behaviour while protecting him from consequences.

Jack* was one such person, a man who was very proud of his nickname. He was 'the Engineer' when he worked at Harrods because of his crucial role in phone bugging. 'Everyone called me it, because I knew about computers and was very technically minded. Even the chairman always called me "the Engineer". I don't think he ever knew my name.

'There were recording devices everywhere, and I'd have to make sure they were working and we were picking up everything clearly. Most of the things we recorded weren't listened to by the chairman, but it was important that we did the recordings and kept everything properly filed, in case he asked.

'I'd get a call saying, "The chairman wants recordings from someone's phone, or he wants to know what was said in a particular meeting room." I had to have the tapes to hand and get them to someone immediately, or the chairman would get cross. I always felt under a lot of pressure to make sure that everything coming in through bugging devices was loud and clear.'

Jack says he bugged everyone from board members, finance directors, the HR directors and management to secretaries, chauffeurs and bodyguards. 'No one was off limits. If he wanted to know what any individual said that morning, I had to be able to tell him. He was the chairman, it was his right to know what was happening in his business.'

Jack didn't have to transcribe the tapes; that was down to a man called Bob Loftus and his senior security operatives. They'd go through the tapes and extract the information that was pertinent, then this would be passed to Fayed. Although Jack played a crucial role in the Fayed set-up, he doesn't think that he 'assisted' Fayed in his criminality. 'I was just doing my job,' he maintains.

He says he had no idea that the information he was passing on would be used for such nefarious means. 'If I hadn't done it, someone else would have,' he says. 'It's not like I could have stopped him. I had no idea of what he was up to or what he was using the tapes for. I thought he was worried about industrial espionage or something, or fraud. I thought maybe that's what business leaders did.'

Many of the Harrods employees I interviewed said the same two things: first, they had no idea of the scale of Fayed's criminality, and second, he would have found someone to do it, so why not them? Why should they not benefit from Fayed's largesse? Such an argument can be used to justify the most heinous of crimes. These people helped Fayed to cause pain and misery. They 'enabled' him – that's precisely the right word. By bowing to his demands and doing his bidding, they helped him to commit crimes.

Many of Fayed's senior staff knew what was going on and positively assisted him. Middle-ranking members of staff might have had their suspicions and did nothing, and younger staff members who had not worked previously could have assumed the role they undertook was common in business and were ignorant about the consequences.

'Biggie' insists that he and others working in security were in this last category; they had no idea what was going on. Whether or not this is believable, given the amount of access they had to Fayed, is debatable. But, as time went on, we can be sure that it was certainly not true of those at the top of the security operation, nor was it true of those in administrative jobs, who saw the paperwork and processed the complaints and resignation letters from those who were leaving because they'd been abused by Fayed.

If you take a moment to ponder just how many people were involved in every one of Fayed's vile acts, it's astonishing to consider how far the deception of so many people went. The personal assistants who called the women to Fayed's office and apartment and watched them return, pained and crying; the security guards who protected the apartment where he carried out many of the attacks and ignored the girls' screams; the doctors, the phone operators, the senior executives . . . many knew, and most suspected. They might not have known the extent of it, but they were aware that something was going on. And it doesn't stop there. There was so much involvement from so many people.

One of these people was Kelly Walker-Duncalf, whom we've already encountered several times in previous chapters. Walker-Duncalf was a shop-floor worker who rose to become head of store approvals and a firm Fayed ally with the ultimate say in who worked at the store. She hunted for women who could be 'chairman's girls'.

Walker-Duncalf started working at Harrods in 1997, aged nineteen. Her career began on the shop floor in the menswear concession, and by 2000 she'd been promoted to buyer's clerk in men's tailoring. Then she was given a huge promotion, to head of store approvals in 2003, a hugely powerful role that gave the final say-so over the hiring of staff. She worked in a building across from the main Harrods store, and spent a decade overseeing the types of women who came to work in Harrods, ensuring they were the 'right type'. Her department was responsible for vetting new recruits and maintaining standards for the company.

The position gave her extensive influence over hiring decisions and a direct line to Fayed, with whom she'd developed a close relationship. She was aware of exactly what sort of women and girls he liked, and she went out of her way to find precisely those who fitted the brief. She conducted store walks to hunt for potential victims; these walks were supposed to be an opportunity for Walker-Duncalf to check that staff were dressed appropriately and were interacting with customers. Instead, she scanned the sea of faces and bodies, looking for targets. She instructed senior staff to take Polaroid pictures of the most attractive women in their departments, which she would then go through. She also handed out business cards to young women in bars, pubs and even on the street, encouraging them to come into Harrods and meet the chairman.

JESS

It was a busy Saturday night at a Kensington pub in 2004, and Jess* was enjoying a night out with friends. She went up to the bar, ordered a tray of shots and reached into her bag to pay for them.

'But before I could hand over the money, the barman told me that the drinks had been paid for. He pointed to the end of the bar, where a really attractive woman was sitting. At first I thought she was a TV presenter. She had the right look – glossy and blonde.

'She walked over and introduced herself, and said she hoped I didn't mind her buying the drinks. I said that I never minded people buying drinks for me. She said her name was Kelly Walker-Duncalf, and she worked at Harrods, directly for Mohamed Al-Fayed, and she could get me and my friends jobs there. I guess I'd had a few to drink by then, so I invited her to join us. I told her I'd get her a shot as well, but she didn't want one.

'When we got over to the table, she said, "You could make loads of money at Harrods and have a brilliant career, working in fashion." We would only have been about eighteen, I guess she was a few years older – probably in her late twenties – but so well put together. I thought it all sounded amazing. I was working in a bar in East London at the time. I loved the thought of this glamorous life.

'She also said she could introduce us to rich business-men. She said the richest men in the world went to Harrods and they were always looking for pretty girls to spend money on. We were flattered. I thought she was genuine.'

Jess went into Harrods a few days later to find out more about the job on offer. She says Walker-Duncalf had told her exactly how to dress and how to behave. 'I got there and there was no sign of Kelly, but people knew who I was and I was offered a job. I texted Kelly to tell her, and she replied to say she'd introduce me to the chairman when I went in.'

Jess reported for work the following week, as instructed, and was met by Walker-Duncalf. 'She looked more glamorous than ever, with perfect nails and blow-dry, and immaculate make-up. She took me to meet Mohamed Al-Fayed at his apartment before anything else. He seemed nice, and told me to come with him. He led me to a bathroom, told me to brush my teeth and said that I could take a shower if I wanted to. He added that when I'd finished brushing my teeth, I was to throw the brush into the bin.

'It's odd what you do when you're young and in the company of someone like that, but I didn't understand what was happening, so I brushed my teeth and walked back out. He was waiting, and pushed me towards a bedroom and pulled me onto the bed. He said we could talk while lying down, then he reached over and pushed his hand inside my blouse. I pushed him off and tried to sit up, but he held me down and tried to kiss me. I wriggled away but he was so strong, and kept pulling me back.

'He stuck his tongue into my mouth and had a hand up my skirt. It was awful. I was only just eighteen, and he was this horrible old man. When I got away, I ran for the door and banged on it until someone let me out.'

As soon as Jess was out of the room, she phoned Walker-Duncalf, who, she assumed, would be appalled by what had happened. But she got no such reaction. 'Kelly told me I was ridiculous, and I should have let him do whatever he wanted to. He was the richest man in the world, women everywhere wanted to sleep with him. She sounded very cross.'

Jess says that Walker-Duncalf had made such an impression on her that she felt guilty. She even sent her a text saying, 'I'm sorry I let you down.'

'Next time will be better,' came the reply.

Jess says that the next time she was attacked, Walker-Duncalf was in the apartment while Fayed grabbed and groped her in his bedroom. She let him tear her clothes off and digitally rape her while she cried. Then she got up and walked back into the apartment where Walker-Duncalf was sitting.

'He handed Kelly an envelope that was stuffed full of money – there must have been thousands in there. She turned to me and said, "You will have one of these if you let him have sex with you." It was the worst experience of my life. When I think about it all now, it's clear that she set up the whole thing. I bet she's done it dozens of times before.'

Walker-Duncalf left Harrods in 2013, the same year that she and Fayed were arrested and interviewed after a woman called Francesca reported Fayed for rape and Walker-Duncalf for aiding him. The case was dropped by the Crown Prosecution Service.

Walker-Duncalf worked at Selfridges, then set up her own recruitment company called Solutions, based in Hanover Square, described as 'one of London's most exclusive post boats'. Today she lives in Jersey and did not respond when approached to comment.

JOY

Joy was a young woman who went to Paris with Fayed. She thought she was there to help organise meetings for him, but when she arrived she realised there were already three PAs in situ. She spoke to Fayed and asked him what he wanted her to do on the trip.

'I'll tell you when we get in the car,' he said.

Once they were underway, he showed her. He grabbed her and groped her, tearing at her clothes and forcing her to kiss him while she screamed as loudly as she could and attempted to fight him off. The chauffeur, one of Fayed's regular drivers, drove on. Let's not pretend that he didn't know what was happening on the back seats. Joy tried to talk to the chauffeur later that day, and begged him to help her, but he simply walked away.

Joy was raped in her room that night. The bedroom door didn't lock and the electricity didn't work. She was stuck in a cold, dark room and suffered the most horrific abuse. Two security officers stood outside the room all the time. They all have blood on their hands.

The haunting question that emerges from cases like Fayed's is why so many witnesses remained silent. We'd all like to think that, in similar circumstances, we'd speak out to protect someone who was being attacked. But contemporary research in social psychology suggests that we might not, especially in corporate or team environments because of the phenomenon that's known as 'ethical fading'. This is when ethical principles stop mattering in big organisations because people see everything in terms of the business and no longer think about the moral dimensions.

Another term for this is 'moral disengagement'. This theory suggests that personal morality disappears in an organisation for four reasons:

1. **Displacement of responsibility** ('Security handles these matters')
2. **Diffusion of responsibility** ('Everyone saw it happening')
3. **Advantageous comparison** ('At least they have jobs')
4. **Dehumanisation of victims** ('They're just gold-diggers')

Another factor that's pertinent here is what's known as the 'bystander effect'. This is something that people have been aware of since the 1960s, when two scientists, John M. Darley and Bibb Latané, began work on the idea. Their research shows that people tend to be inhibited from helping in an emergency situation as a result of the presence of other people, particularly when their own position is subordinate within a hierarchy.

The chauffeur who drove while Joy was assaulted in the back of the car is an example of this. The driver was a professional bystander, which means he amended his perceptions of the event and convinced himself that he didn't hear screams or didn't understand what was happening because of the environment he was in – doing his job with his boss in the car. In any other circumstance he may have done something, but in that moment, in a normal work situation, he didn't act, remaining a bystander to the entire event.

This widespread predisposition is augmented by what's known as 'moral creep', which means that the small adjustments we make in a work environment, such as ignoring a suggestive comment or smiling at an offensive gesture, create permission for accepting increasingly severe violations of widely accepted norms. The moral lines shift gradually, without anyone realising, until it eventually feels acceptable for management to behave in an appalling way. It's down to the leader of an organisation to set the culture, and the leader in this story had a very peculiar idea of what constituted culture. It didn't seem to occur to him that morality was in any way important. People became used to a lack of morality and were immune to its dangers.

Clearly, those at the top of the organisation should have been working to prevent dangerous situations from arising and create a safe psychological space for workers. They should have been confronting Fayed, but if they had, they would have been sacked on some trumped-up charge. And they knew that, so they too kept quiet.

Also, many were victims of the 'Lucifer Effect', whereby institutions transform ordinary individuals into enablers of evil: 'systems create hierarchies of dominance with influence and communication going down, rarely up,' according to social psychologist Philip Zimbardo. This materialised in Harrods. Fayed would try to turn his senior employees into 'Lucifers' to make them more vulnerable and compliant.

Jon Brilliant, a Harrods director who joined the store in 2000, recalls that he was indoctrinated into this system as soon as he started. Shortly before his first business trip to Microsoft in Seattle, Fayed presented him with a brown envelope containing $5,000 in $50 notes. When Brilliant later attempted to return the untouched funds, Fayed refused to accept them, asking pointedly, 'You didn't need any entertainment?' This pattern continued over subsequent months, with Brilliant receiving large-denomination notes ahead of business travels.

Brilliant was well aware of Fayed's true intentions: 'He was trying to get you to come back and say, "Oh, I spent money on drugs or I spent money frolicking, doing something that I shouldn't have been doing." Then he had you, and he would use that information against you should you ever turn on him. I am certainly aware of people who . . . succumbed to the temptation.'

This manufacturing of compromising situations that create psychological debt and dependency was something that Fayed appeared to do instinctively, knowing that it gave him ultimate power. It was one of the reasons for his use of such extensive surveillance. If he heard someone say something incriminating, he'd be delighted.

Brilliant believes his communications were monitored by Fayed's extensive security apparatus. 'Even when I tell this story to you right now, I get kind of goosebumps and the hair stands up on the back of my neck, realising that my phones were being listened in on,' he says. He recalls words from a private phone conversation being quoted back to him during a meeting, confirming his suspicions that he was being spied on.

Brilliant's workspace existed within what he describes as Fayed's 'ring of steel' office suite on Harrods's fifth floor, protected by two sets of security doors. There, administrative assistants – all young, blonde and attractive – served their master obediently.

The Metropolitan Police is now looking closely at whether those individuals who assisted Fayed committed any criminal offence. Officers are reported to have already spoken to five people about their work for Fayed.

Richard Meeran is from law firm Leigh Day, representing many of the women abused by Fayed. He's adamant that the involvement of other people in the organisation was key to Fayed being able to abuse on the scale he did. He says it's not just a case of people turning 'a blind eye' – there were lots of people actively involved in helping Fayed. According to Meeran, '[Fayed] was the head of a deeply criminal organisation who relied on a team of enablers to silence his victims.'

While the surveillance teams and human resources staff facilitated Fayed's abuse from within, another layer of protection came from those tasked with managing his public image. These people were the buffer between his private depravity and public scrutiny. One of the principal players on this stage was Michael Cole. If you heard anything about Fayed in the 1980s or 90s, chances are that it came through Cole. The man spoke so lovingly, for so long, about someone so deplorable, that one must assume that he was driven mad by the role and had taken leave of his senses. Or it was because of the vast amount of money on offer. Cole was paid an estimated £1 million for turning up whenever his presence was required and reframing Fayed's nonsense into bite-sized chunks for the media.

Cole would issue harshly worded denials on those occasions when the media stepped out of line, and he made sure that the best spin possible accompanied Fayed's every public appearance. He was a key line of defence, the protector of Fayed's reputation, and there's no question that he played his part in shielding the world from the truth of Fayed's life. This cognitive dissonance was staggering. Exercising 'doublethink' to a world record-breaking degree, he was able to forget any fact that had become inconvenient.

No one wishes to make any comparisons between Hitler and Fayed, but the process of self-deception bears comparison.

A number of the medical professionals who experimented on inmates at Nazi concentration and death camps were studied by Robert Jay Lifton, who identified a process that he called 'doubling' – the creation of a second self that could perform evil, allowing the primary self to maintain its moral identity. His research found that these professionals didn't simply become monsters; they developed psychological mechanisms that enabled them to participate in atrocities while still seeing themselves as decent people. Again, there's no suggestion that comparisons can be made between Harrods and Nazi Germany, but the research highlights issues that may be considered pertinent to our understanding of events that unfolded at the store.

When Fayed died in August 2023, Cole was the first to comment, gushing freely about his late chairman, who was, apparently, 'fascinating, larger than life, full of great humanity'. That might not be how many of us will remember him, but Cole was always verbose when talking about Fayed and he remained like that until the news about Fayed's rapes and abuse came to light.

Then the rhetoric stopped. There was no more praise. In fact, there was no more anything. The man simply disappeared. Like Lord Lucan before him, he has been neither seen nor heard from since. Calls to his mobile go unanswered and calls to his home are taken by his wife, who declares that the man of the house is unavailable for comment. Perhaps he's still grief-stricken at Fayed's death. Or perhaps he's hiding away as the truth comes tumbling out.

Cole defended Fayed against allegations made about his impropriety in Maureen Orth's 1995 article in *Vanity Fair* and in Tom Bower's excellent *Fayed: The Unauthorized Biography*, published three years later.

When Sophia Money-Coutts went to interview Fayed in 2014, Cole asked her to omit any 'banter' from her story. Cole warned her that 'Mr Al Fayed is going to take one look at you and say something to the effect of, "Will you be my third wife?" So could I please have your assurance that none of this light-hearted banter will make it into your article?' If the whole story weren't so utterly awful, we might pause at this point to laugh at the madness of it all.

Fayed's media team expanded over time, just as the extent of his criminal activity grew ever greater, with such PR and media luminaries as Conor Nolan, Laurie Mayer and Chester Stern joining his staff. There's no suggestion that these people were aware of what Fayed was up to, but their presence in the story is key because they gave Fayed a respectable public persona while the grim reality festered just below the surface.

Another public relations expert who worked with Fayed was Max Clifford, the renowned publicist and convicted sex criminal, who died in 2017. Clifford confided to journalist Chris Atkins how much Fayed, then seventy-six, loved girls in their teens. 'He's a randy old sod,' he said. 'But if he is groping seventeen-year-olds that are quite willing because they are being paid a lot of money – fine.'

Fayed contributed £250,000 every year to the Shooting Star CHASE hospice, where Clifford served as patron. 'It all works extremely well,' Clifford remarked. But by 2000 charity contributions were no longer enough, and Fayed began to pay Clifford £300,000 per year.

* * *

The #MeToo movement has been astonishing in revealing what happens when women speak out – transformation occurs. Evil thrives in the shadows and shrivels in the light. Once vast numbers of women started telling the truth of their experiences, the wall of secrecy crashed down. We are moving into an era in which powerful men are finding it increasingly difficult to prey on women with impunity.

James Baldwin once wrote, 'Not everything that is faced can be changed, but nothing can be changed until it is faced.' In confronting Harrods's toxic legacy, these testimonies force society to face uncomfortable truths about power, complicity and the systems that have long silenced victims.

Many of the women I spoke to talked of feeling a sense of having been duped when they watched the BBC documentary. By not speaking out at the time, they felt they were part of an enabling culture that allowed a very rich, powerful man to commit monstrous acts without consequence. Many were frustrated and disappointed with themselves, with a sense of guilt that they didn't do more to address the problem at the time and thus make it safer for those women coming after them.

It was, however, so difficult to challenge anything in the prevailing climate. Culturally and socially, it was a different time. Women hesitated to challenge workplace misogyny, knowing they risked being labelled troublesome or losing their job altogether. The women working at Harrods didn't stand a chance against a billionaire with an army of lawyers at his disposal.

So, finally, what of the women who helped Fayed? Abigail, who worked at Harrods during the 1990s, says she finds the fact that women helped him too unbearable to forgive. 'As a female, you grow up thinking a man might hurt you. I'm sorry that sounds harsh, but you take precautions with men that you would never take with a woman. Men are stronger. If a woman attacked me, I'd have a fighting chance, but not with a man. So, the thought of a man attacking you, helped by a woman who lures you in – that's just awful.'

The most shocking recent example of a woman helping a man to attack other women is of course Ghislaine Maxwell. The Oxford-educated daughter of disgraced media tycoon Robert Maxwell operated as Jeffrey Epstein's chief enabler, recruiting vulnerable young women and girls for him. She was a refined, well-connected woman who could disarm suspicions that might otherwise have been raised by a lone middle-aged man approaching teenage girls. What makes Maxwell's case particularly disturbing is the extent of her betrayal of her own gender. Court testimony revealed how she presented herself as a mentor figure to these girls before delivering them into Epstein's hands.

In 2021 she was convicted on five counts relating to sex trafficking. Judge Alison Nathan, in sentencing Maxwell to twenty years in prison, said: 'Ms. Maxwell directly and repeatedly and over the course of many years participated in a horrific scheme to entice, transport and traffic under-age girls, some as young as fourteen.'

Abigail says that there were women positioned all the way along her path to being abused. 'A woman in Harrods showed me to my desk, and a woman instructed me to go for a medical examination. The horrible, intrusive medical was conducted by a woman, and it was a woman who called me in to see Fayed. Are you saying that not one woman in that line-up knew what would happen to me. Not one?'

Equally troubling is the apparent absence of investigation by Harrods itself. Despite numerous allegations spanning decades, researchers have found no evidence that the store conducted any formal inquiry while Fayed remained chairman. There seemed to be a complete moral disengagement from what was going on.

James McArthur, who served as CEO in 2008, told BBC interviewers that he had no recollection of Fayed being interviewed by police that year regarding allegations of sexual assault on a fifteen-year-old girl. Also, he did not recall television news crews outside Harrods reporting on the very serious allegations that the company chairman had abused a child.

This pattern of strategic blindness reveals the most disturbing truth about institutional abuse: it requires not only active perpetrators but an entire ecosystem of enablers, from those who directly facilitate to those who simply choose not to see.

The Fayed case demonstrates how power corrupts not just the powerful but those in their orbit, creating circles of complicity that extend far beyond the central abuser. As investigations continue and more executives face questioning, perhaps the most important question is not just who knew what, but how we dismantle the systems that allow such wilful blindness to flourish and persist in the corridors of wealth and influence.

16

THE CROWN FIXATION

'How long do you think we've got today?
Four or five minutes?'

Princess Diana to the security guards at Harrods,
mocking how quickly Fayed would appear on
realising that she had arrived

For a man who started life selling fizzy drinks from an Egyptian street, Fayed developed a remarkably elaborate thirst for royal approval. The self-styled 'Mohamed of the Glen' pursued Britain's most exclusive family with the tenacity of a terrier. The royal family was the epitome of Britishness and he longed to be associated with them, whatever it took.

Fayed claimed that his obsession with the royal family began in his youth, once claiming that the abdication of Edward VIII in 1936 'had a big influence on me', a curious admission, especially since he was only seven years old at the time. It was the year in which he lost his mother, so one suspects he had other concerns, but it suits Fayed to announce this early interest in the royals.

It wasn't until he was ensconced in Harrods that he was able to start courting every available royal connection in the hope of befriending the Windsors. His first major move came in 1986, following the death of Wallis Simpson, the

American divorcée for whom Edward VIII had abandoned the throne. Fayed took over the lease of the Villa Windsor in Paris and poured millions into restoring the property to its former glory, hoping that it would be the perfect place for members of the royal family to visit him. Fayed offered Queen Elizabeth II the table on which her uncle had signed his abdication document, but she had the sense to turn it down. Nothing came without cost with Fayed.

Patrick Jephson, Princess Diana's former private secretary, said, 'Fayed was an intensely theatrical character who understood the persuasive power of largesse. His generosity to members of the royal family was calculated to foster a sense of obligation.' The Queen, however, had seen through it, so Fayed kept hold of his table. He now needed a new approach, deciding to work his way through Diana's side of the family, whom he figured might be easier to convince.

Fayed cultivated a relationship with Diana's father Earl Spencer and her stepmother Raine, Countess Spencer, who was eventually appointed to the Harrods board of directors. As well as befriending the Spencers, Fayed invited Prince and Princess Michael of Kent to his Surrey estate. As for Diana herself, she was always welcome in Harrods. Whenever she visited she was told to use Door 11, the most discreet entrance. Every time she'd check her watch as she walked through the door, wondering how long it would be before Fayed rushed to her side.

Biggie remembers her talking to security guards about it. 'The guys on the door said she was lovely, and were always joking about how quickly the boss would arrive when she walked into the store. She would ask them, "How long do you think we've got today? Four or five minutes?" They always laughed, then minutes later, the chairman was there, smiling and thrilled to see her. Perhaps she didn't realise that it was exactly those bodyguards who were telling him that she was there.'

Fayed first asked Diana to join him on holiday on his yacht years before she actually went. In 1990, when she was still married to Charles, he suggested that she join him and his family in France, but when Diana asked her security to fly to France to check how safe it was, they replied that it seemed neither safe nor appropriate for her to go.

Meanwhile, Fayed kept up the fight to win the affection of the royal family, with no detail being too small in Fayed's royal charm offensive. Royal staff who were introduced to him at official engagements would find Harrods Gold Cards, personalised with their names, delivered to them by courier. This calculated generosity extended to the royals themselves.

'Every time Mr Fayed appeared at a royal event, there would be an audible groan among the staff. His eagerness to please was exhausting,' a former Buckingham Palace staff member said. 'He'd be dismissive of most staff he came across, but when they were linked to the royal family it was a different thing. He was practically bowing to them just because of their closeness to royalty.'

Fayed sent horse-drawn Harrods vans to Kensington Palace filled with gifts for Diana and her sons. These deliveries became so frequent that on one occasion, as the distinctive green and gold van approached, she reportedly asked the driver with weary resignation, 'Is this from Mr Fayed? Oh dear.'

Fayed's most successful royal networking venture was Harrods's sponsorship of the Royal Windsor Horse Show and the sport of polo, both of which brought him into regular contact with the Queen and Prince Philip. But their encounters didn't always go well. In 1993 Prince Philip mentioned his arthritis during a conversation with Fayed. Feeling the need to be helpful, Fayed began undressing, and explained that his shirtmaker Turnbull & Asser, a company he owned, produced shirts secured with Velcro, as well clip-on ties; these were 'a godsend for men with stiff joints'. To demonstrate, he whipped off his own clip-on tie and dramatically ripped open the Velcro placket on his shirt while courtiers rushed to stop him.

'Everybody knew what his game was,' one former royal aide later recalled. 'He wanted to be part of the country's elite. That was fine. As long as you dealt with him with your eyes wide open, he was no more of a rogue than a lot of other people who were hanging around London at the time. Certainly, he brightened up the palace when he came, with his funny ways and inability to understand the most basic etiquette and protocols. I'm still dining out on the time he started undressing in front of Her Majesty.'

Once Diana had separated from Charles and was free to make her own decisions about where – and with whom – she spent her time, Fayed cosied in with another offer of hospitality. 'Come to the south of France,' he suggested in 1997 after a formal dinner at the Churchill Hotel in Portman Square. 'Bring the boys. I fly you down. You have your own house by the sea with swimming pool. Very private. You need a holiday.'

But Inspector Ken Wharfe, Diana's bodyguard, was worried: 'His reputation was already controversial and I was very anxious that Diana associating with him would not only harm her, but the good name of the monarchy. I told her that he was basically a villain, and it would make life very difficult for the Queen if he was able to parade the princess and the boys as his guests at a time when he was publicly fighting Her Majesty's government over its failure to grant him a passport.'

Dai Davies, Scotland Yard's former head of royal protection, who was in charge of keeping the royals safe from 1994 to 1998, said he was aware of allegations that Fayed had 'a reputation', and warned royal officials that Scotland Yard's Serious and Organised Crime Command was investigating him. He remembers warning the palace about Fayed's reputation as 'a salacious attacker of women'. 'There were allegations I was aware of that Fayed had sexually assaulted women, then paid them off,' Davies said. 'I had no compunction in warning the Queen about this individual.' Davies was told that the palace was aware of the allegations.

Diana's friends were equally horrified that Diana and her sons were planning to spend time with Fayed. They were worried that she'd be used by him for photo opportunities and were at pains to point out that all of Fayed's properties were wired, so everything she said and did would be transmitted straight back to him.

Indeed, there was only one person urging Diana to go to France that summer: Raine, her stepmother, with whom she had reconciled after a difficult period. Raine was a director of Harrods – what a brilliant power move by Fayed – so had become a fan. Diana therefore decided to take the boys on holiday on Fayed's yacht that summer. Fayed rang his eldest son and told him to come quickly to the mooring. Despite Dodi being engaged to Kelly Fisher and preparing for his wedding, his father told him to befriend Diana, saying that she was exactly the sort of women he should be dating.

Dodi rushed to the yacht, and a romance developed between him and Diana, though there's no indication that it was a serious relationship, despite Fayed's claims. She certainly wasn't pregnant when she died, and there's no indication that an engagement ring had been bought. They'd only known each other for a few weeks.

None of this mattered in the slightest to Fayed. He was ecstatic, jubilant at what he saw as his final triumph over the Establishment. The mother of a future king was in his family. They were outsiders no longer.

So the car crash in Paris that killed both Diana and Dodi on 31 August 1997 didn't just take Fayed's son; it took Fayed's future, the future he'd always dreamed of for himself and his family. He became convinced that the royal family, particularly Prince Philip, had orchestrated the deaths to prevent Diana from marrying a Muslim and bearing his grandchild. He was furious. Wracked with grief and torn apart by what felt like another rejection by the royal family after years of being an outcast, he turned on them with accusations of the most vile nature, accusing them of murdering his son and 'future daughter-in-law'. While he insulted the royal family, stories leaked out about the royal family's view of him. First a report that Prince Philip had referred to Dodi Fayed as an 'oily bed-hopper'. Then stories that the royal family had a meeting at Balmoral at which MI6 presented a special report on the Fayeds. Later, a biography of Diana by Tina Brown revealed that the princess 'had no intention of marrying Dodi Fayed but had a dalliance with him merely to annoy Charles and the Royal Family'.

Fayed continued his very public mourning of his son. He commissioned the gaudy memorial to Diana and Dodi at Harrods, which appeared in the store the year after the 1997 car crash. This controversial tribute, lovingly created by Fayed, featured a wine glass smudged with Diana's lipstick that was purportedly used by her during her final dinner at the Ritz in Paris. It also contained Dodi's cigarette from their 'last meal', along with a statue called *Innocent Victims* showing the couple dancing beneath the wings of an albatross. The word 'Innocent' was presumably chosen to reinforce Fayed's conspiracy theory about their deaths.

Most controversially, the memorial featured the 'engagement ring' that Dodi allegedly purchased for Diana shortly before their deaths, even though no one else in the couple's family or social circle seems to know anything about this pending engagement.

In 2005 an additional piece appeared: an elaborate bronze statue sculpted by Bill Mitchell (Fayed's personal designer) at the base of the Egyptian escalator. The life-sized bronze showed the couple dancing through water, with their clothes flowing around them.

The memorials remained in place until 2018, when the new Qatari owners removed them and returned the statue to the Fayed family. The statue now sits in Fayed's family home in Surrey.

Fayed's tribute to Dodi and Diana, while representing his love for his late son, was also a further reminder of his strength of feeling towards the royal family. His move from an 'obsession' with them, to accusing them of murder and having a deep mistrust and dislike of them, was a spine running through the back of everything he did.

He threw himself into a battle against the royal family for the rest of his life. Prince Philip stripped Harrods of its prestigious royal warrants in January 2000 and the Queen switched her annual order of 1,000 Harrods Christmas puddings to the supermarket chain Tesco. They wanted nothing more to do with Fayed, not that they'd ever been keen on him in the first place. He was an outsider, and would always remain an outsider.

It wasn't until 2008, when the inquest he'd campaigned for concluded that the crash had been an accident, that he finally let up. But even then he could not bow out with dignity. 'I'm leaving the rest for God to get my revenge,' he said.

17

BROTHERS IN ARMS

THE FAYED SIBLINGS

'He was really angry – snarling and shouting and telling me never, ever to block him from entering a room in his hotel again.'

Lila on her attempts to keep Fayed
out of her hotel room in Paris

LILA

Lila* is the most reluctant of all the interviewees that I've spoken to. She agrees to talk, then changes her mind, agrees again, then worries about whether she should speak out. Eventually she calls and says that she's been thinking about it and wants to offer her story because it's important.

'We can't help future generations, and we can't change anything, if we don't speak out,' she says. 'We sat in silence and said nothing when he was alive. What's the excuse for staying silent now? Nothing excuses apathy now.' Her bravery, like that of all the women who have shared their stories here, is remarkable.

She went to work for Fayed in 1990, in the beauty hall. Her story begins in a similar fashion to others – she was spotted by him when he was on a walk through the store and found herself being lured to a job in his office, with promises of a role in the buying department, the carrot dangled above the heads of so many of the woman he took a liking to.

Once she was ensconced in his office, the requests for her to come and see him began. 'He'd make me come in, tell me how beautiful I was, make some smutty comment, and give me money. He said the money was for me to buy new clothes, and he told me not to buy a handbag with it, because he had one he wanted to give me.'

This sounds like a lovely situation – who wouldn't want to be lavished with money and expensive bags? But Lila says it was never right, and the whole thing made her feel tense and awkward. 'It always felt as if he would want something in exchange for the money. It never felt like a gift. The whole thing made me very nervous. I even kept the money in an envelope so that I could return it if I needed to. I always had this odd idea that he would accuse me of stealing it, or tell me it was payment for something. I didn't like it.'

The handbag that was presented to her was beautiful, but – again – she felt herself stiffen when he handed it over and asked her to 'give Papa a kiss'. It was a Chloé bag that was the 'It' bag at the time, and he expected her to be grateful rather than terrified out of her mind. 'He told me to relax and began to massage my shoulders. Then he told me that I must bring the bag when we went to Paris. Paris? I had no idea we were going to Paris.'

Fayed explained that they needed to go to the Ritz for meetings later that day. Lila said she needed to go home to collect her things, but he said that wasn't necessary – she could take whatever she needed from the store. He added that they were only going for one day, so she wouldn't need much.

'I'd hoped to get out of going. I'd met a really nice guy and we were due to be going out that evening. I was excited about the date and though going to Paris was a lovely thing to do, I was extremely worried about the chairman by this stage – I didn't want his gifts, his money or anything.'

However much she disliked Fayed, she had no idea about how bad things would get. She travelled to Paris separately from him, without a clue about what would be expected from her when she arrived. 'I thought maybe I'd have to take notes in meetings or make arrangements for him. I steeled myself; it was only for one afternoon – I could cope.'

When she arrived at the Ritz she joined Fayed and another man for coffee, and sat in silence while they spoke to one another in what she imagines was Arabic. 'I'd not heard him do that before. It felt very rude, and I had a horrible feeling they were talking about me. The other man was staring at my chest the whole time. He never introduced himself, and Fayed never introduced him.

'Fayed asked whether I had my handbag with me. I did have it, but only because he'd given it to me that morning and I'd come straight from work. He said, "Good girl. I knew you loved it and I know you love me." The other man laughed and nodded ferociously. I didn't particularly love the bag and I definitely didn't love him.'

Lila takes breaks while we talk, standing up and walking around the coffee shop, trying to gather her thoughts before we continue. We'd originally planned to meet in her flat but she said she didn't want the memories to be churned up there so asked whether I could choose a café instead, one that she'd never been to before and was unlikely to go to again.

When she sits back down, she gets to the crux of the story. Fayed told her that they'd have to stay overnight. He had business meetings in the morning and needed to be in Paris. She asked whether she could leave, but he said no, she was needed at the meetings. That evening, after a very awkward dinner with Fayed, during which he tried to encourage her to drink and kept telling her to relax, and said he knew how to relax her – they'd make love later, then she'd feel much better – she went up to her room and discovered there was no lock on the door.

She called down to reception and explained in broken French that there was no lock. They said simply that was the room she was in. Mr Fayed had chosen it. 'I felt,' she recalls, 'like I'd been punched in the stomach.'

She tried to sleep that night, but was fearful that Fayed would come in. Why else would he put her in a room without a lock on the door? Her worst nightmares came true at around 1 a.m., when he pushed the door open, swearing and shouting as he pushed past the chairs she'd piled in front of the door.

'He was really angry – snarling and shouting and telling me never, ever to block him from entering a room in his hotel again. Then he pushed me back against the bed and began tearing my clothes off. I was wearing my day clothes because I had no nightwear with me, and didn't want to go to bed naked in case he came in.

'He raped me, and I blacked out. I don't know why. For years I thought that he put a cloth of some sort over my mouth with a chemical to knock me out, but I'm not sure whether that's the case. I actually don't remember, and I don't remember now why I thought that.

'I've been thinking hard about what happened so I can tell you everything I know. The only facts I know for sure are that he came into the room, he was really angry that I'd tried to keep him out, and then he climbed onto the bed and held me down and was forcing my legs open. Then next thing I know, I woke up.'

She looked over and Fayed was in the bed next to her. She recalls sitting up, her head pounding, feeling sick and hurting everywhere. She felt like she'd been in a car crash. 'I couldn't stop shaking but I knew I had to get out of the room, so I looked around and tried to find my clothes. It took me a few minutes to realise they weren't there because I was in a different room. That's when the terror really set in. I actually didn't know where I was.

'I grabbed a towel from the bathroom and ran towards the door. When I looked at Fayed in the bed, I realised that it wasn't him there, but the rude Egyptian man I'd met earlier. I later found out that he was Salah, the brother.'

Lila left the room, and as she ran down the corridor, unsure where she was going, she realised she was bleeding.

Blood was running down her legs as she stepped into the lift and went down to the reception area. 'I tried to explain that I needed help. I needed them to call the police and I needed to go to hospital, but they either realised what had happened and didn't want to help, or they didn't know what I was talking about. Either way, I was alone and scared. I told them that they must know which room I had been in because I phoned down to complain about the room having no lock. "That's where my clothes are," I screamed.

'The women behind the reception were talking to one another in French and moved to make a phone call. I screamed. "Don't call him." The woman put the phone down, and I sat down on one of those elaborate gold chairs and wept.

'Then a woman appeared. She'd been up to the room and got my things for me. She took me through reception and told me to get changed. She called a cab for me and I left. I decided to go back to London before calling the police, but by the time I got home I felt so ill I couldn't face it.

'I went back to my mum's house and said I was unwell. I also said that I was going to leave the job because I didn't like it. I never told her what happened, and I never told the police. I told my husband about five years ago. He's the guy who I was supposed to go on that first date with on the night I was taken to Paris, so that worked out, but life's been extremely difficult.

'I refused to be intimate with him for years. I'm lucky he put up with me. I'd like to say I'm much better now, but

I'm really not. I've met up with other people who were attacked by Fayed, but no one else I know was attacked by both brothers. I can still feel the terror of realising I was in a different room, and seeing Salah in the bed. Sometimes I don't know how I coped. I don't know how I've come to this place where I now have a "normal" life, despite what he did.'

Maria Mulla, the barrister representing the Justice for Harrods Survivors, says they are investigating accusations against Salah, who died in 2010.

HELEN

Lila's story is so horrific that it's hard to imagine the pain and misery that she went through. The frightening thing is that research indicates that she's not the first person to have been attacked by two of the brothers. And there are others who also believe they were drugged, like her.

Fayed spotted Helen on one of his daily walks around the Harrods shop floor, and he moved her up to his offices where she would work as a personal assistant. She had a call one day to say that she needed to accompany the chairman on a business trip to Dubai and Abu Dhabi in February 1989. A big group of people were heading out there, and she was flattered to be invited.

But things started to unravel almost immediately. First of all, she discovered that she had been booked to travel alone with Fayed and to stay in his hotel suite, while the rest of the party were staying in different accommodation. There were separate bedrooms and bathrooms in the suite, but Helen knew she was far too close to Fayed for comfort and was concerned that no one else in the party was staying with them.

On the first evening, Helen was in her bathroom getting ready for bed, looking into the mirror, when Fayed appeared behind her without warning. 'It was like out of a horror film. I was in my nightie and he grabbed my hand, started pulling me out the bathroom. I was really trying to stop him, but I couldn't,' she told the BBC. Despite her attempts to push him off, he managed to take her into his room, shove her so hard that she fell back onto the bed and climb on top of her. 'He raped me that night,' she says.

In the morning Helen was so frightened of Fayed, and so scared to be far from home, that she didn't say anything to anyone. She just wanted to go home. When Fayed asked her to sign an NDA a few months after the trip, she did so. She didn't want to anger Fayed, and she had no desire to talk about what happened, so she signed the non-disclosure agreement and pushed it to the back of her mind. She began to look for a new job away from the Knightsbridge store. She wanted a job in which she'd never have to see Fayed again.

Then, out of the blue, a message came through that Fayed would like her to do some secretarial work for his brother Salah at his Park Lane home. This felt like a perfect arrangement. She'd be working in the same area of London but wouldn't have to see Fayed every day. She'd met Salah before, and found him friendly and approachable. He seemed softer than his elder brother and would be much easier to work for.

She went to his offices and began to provide the secretarial assistance he needed. After working hard for a couple of days, before she returned to her day job at Harrods, Salah told her to relax and join him for a glass of champagne. 'Within a few sips I was starting to feel a bit groggy, but I can't describe it as drunk. It was a really dizzy and weird feeling. I wasn't feeling right.'

While Helen sat there, feeling woozy and not knowing why, Salah put on some music in the background and began to cosy up to her. Next, he urged her to have 'just one puff' of a bong he held out. Helen didn't realise it at the time, but it was crack cocaine. She remembers him saying, 'This will make you feel better.'

She told the BBC that the next thing she remembers is waking up on a settee in a completely different room, with double vision and her whole body shaking. As she got up she noticed her jeans' button was undone and her belt was missing. Salah was sitting at her feet at the time, holding a glass of water and a tablet, looking 'nervous and panicky'.

Helen knew instinctively that she'd been raped, and the feeling of semen between her legs confirmed it. Then she became aware that the semen was not just around her vagina but her rectum as well.

'I knew then what had happened. I knew.'

She was still feeling shaky and uncoordinated after the drugs, so she sat down and tried to calm herself. While she sat there, Salah called Mohamed in front of her to let him know she wouldn't be going to work at Harrods that day after all. Their conversation was full of laughter, and she knew they were talking about her. Mohamed knew everything. He had raped her, then passed her on to his brother.

Helen moved to walk back to her apartment, but the effects of the drugs meant that she couldn't walk properly, so Salah waked with her and suggested they make a stop to visit a friend. Helen was in no state to argue – she could barely walk or talk – so she agreed that they would pop in to see Salah's friend.

When the man opened the door, he said: 'Hi Helen, how are you this morning?' She says she didn't know the man, so Salah explained: 'He saw you last night.' Helen decided to leave. She staggered away and could hear the two men laughing as she left. Helen is sure that Salah's friend also raped her that night while she was unconscious. She is also sure that she was raped vaginally and anally. Shortly after, Helen resigned from Harrods. 'They've stolen a part of me,' she says. 'It's changed the course of my entire life.'

This coordinated system, in which women were effectively 'passed' from one brother to another as if they were property to be shared at will, is a hugely disturbing development of the story. Before his death from pancreatic cancer in 2010, Salah Fayed escaped public accountability. Mohamed, too, died in 2023 before facing justice.

ELLEN

In 1992 a twenty-two-year-old female Harrods employee called Ellen was sexually assaulted by Fayed. 'He made a lunge for me, grabbing my breasts and trying to get his hand up my skirt. I shouted no, and tried to get away, but he held me so tightly he left bruises all over my arm. I pushed and shoved, and at one point pushed at his face with my hand. He didn't like that – he pushed my hand off and told me to leave. I ran out of the room.'

Ellen didn't see Fayed for a few weeks after that and hoped to be able to get away without seeing him again. Then she received a message that she was to go to Paris to work as a personal assistant. 'I panicked. I was going to be alone in Paris with him. God knows what he would do to me.' Ellen says she debated leaving her job, and was incredibly worried about the trip, but then she was told that she would be working for Salah, Mohamed's younger brother. 'I was so relieved, I can't tell you. I felt like this huge weight had been lifted off my shoulders.'

But when she arrived in Paris she discovered that there was very little work to do. Salah said to her, 'We have lots of time to have fun and get to know one another. My brother sent you to me because he says you will be good for me.' Ellen realised that she'd been sent as a 'gift'. 'It became extremely difficult after that,' she says. 'He kept trying to get me to drink, and whatever drink I asked for, an alcoholic one would arrive. Then he told me I had to get into the hot tub with him and he began washing me. He said how tense I was, and told me about how the resin from a tree in Egypt was good for calming nerves and was very good for blood quality and would make my skin glow. He handed me a bong with the resin in it and told me to take it. I tried it and felt awful. I was all over the place. Salah raped me. I discovered afterwards that I'd been taking crack cocaine, and my drinks had contained sleeping pills.'

In her final days at Harrods, Ellen remembers a new girl starting who seemed 'so young and naive', like she'd once been. Finishing a shift together away from the office, Ellen says she confided in her and warned her about Fayed. Looking back, she says she's pleased she did what she could to try to dissuade her from staying. 'I told her he'd be trying to have sex with her, he'd be touching her, putting her under pressure. I did tell her that I'd been raped by him. She looked horrified but I don't know to this day whether she stayed or left.'

Before she left, Ellen says she was given cash, which at the time she thought was a normal severance procedure – now she thinks it was to keep her quiet. She says what she thought would be her dream job ended up leaving her with lifelong trauma.

'It's taken thirty-five years to speak up, that's how frightened I've been of telling anyone,' she says.

'I want to stand up for victims of abuse, whether corporate or domestic, to let them know that they can speak up too.'

JANE DOE

Jane* worked on the sales floor at Harrods when she was nineteen years old. After a few weeks she was 'spotted' by Fayed's keen-eyed assistants and asked to report directly to his office, where she was greeted by the chairman and told that she would be travelling with him aboard a Harrods helicopter and private plane.

And that's when things changed. She claims to have been raped and trafficked by Mohamed Fayed and has filed a legal claim in the United States District Court for the District of Connecticut to compel Ali, his surviving younger brother, to give evidence about his alleged knowledge of the crimes.

The claim is that Ali Fayed has 'unique and critical evidence' to give about a 'more than two-decade-long trafficking scheme that ensnared and irrevocably injured what is reported to be more than 100 women'.

If he's forced to give evidence, it could reveal hundreds more women who have been abused, and provide yet more detail about Fayed's treatment of women.

Jane claims she 'was trafficked over a substantial period of time, raped and brutally abused' and 'was subject to supervision and surveillance'. During this period, she 'interacted with Ali Fayed on multiple occasions'.

While captive, she 'was shown explicit Polaroid photographs, enough to fill a shoebox, of other women or girls who were physically and sexually abused as part of the Harrods trafficking venture'.

'A medical examination not arranged by Harrods after Jane Doe's escape confirmed signs of her physical abuse.'

She had been forced to sign 'an expansive non-disclosure agreement that obligated her not to disclose any information about her employment or abuse, including to law enforcement'.

The filing says that she 'was threatened and harassed and knew that Harrods' head of security, John [Macnamara], had bragged of the family's ability to handle the Metropolitan police and to commit crimes with impunity.'

As a former Harrods director residing in Greenwich, Connecticut, Ali Fayed is being requested to provide testimony for a planned legal case in British courts. If the request succeeds, he may have to surrender documents and undergo a deposition. Ali Fayed faces no criminal accusations and has not addressed requests for comment.

Linda Singer is a former attorney general of the District of Columbia and now represents the claimant. She said: 'This petition is the first action related to the extensive and egregious sex trafficking allegedly carried out over decades by Harrods and Fayed. While it does not pursue claims against Harrods, Fayed, or others who were involved, it seeks evidence related to those claims from the last of the three living Fayed brothers, who we believe is uniquely positioned to testify to who knew what and who did what.'

But Fayed's legal team say there's no legal basis for him to take part in a discovery process, and it claims the filing by Jane Doe 'reeks of a fishing expedition for the English solicitors who are actively soliciting new clients'.

Federal law permits people in the US to be compelled to be deposed or provide information relevant to court cases in other countries under Article 1782 of the United States Code. Fayed's lawyers maintain that the request falls below the legal threshold for applying Article 1782 on a number of different grounds.

Alexander Pencu, Fayed's attorney, states: 'These requests are not only blatantly improper, but a bad faith fishing expedition designed to harass by collecting information that would never be relevant in litigation.'

Fayed's legal response also stated that Jane Doe has provided no 'detail and no allegations to support' the claim that Ali Fayed was a witness to unlawful behaviour while Jane Doe worked at the clothing store.

The litigation is ongoing before District of Connecticut Judge Omar A. Williams.

Ali Fayed ended his directorship at Harrods when the company was purchased in 2010.

CAROL

Carol* began working for Harrods in 1999 and was employed by Fayed for five years. She left the store over twenty years ago, but she still finds it hard to talk about the time she spent there and the horrible situations in which she found herself. 'Most days in that place I was scared for my life; he was terrifying.'

Fayed tried to rape Carol twice. He asked her to meet him in his private offices, then told her to clean herself. He handed her a bottle of Dettol and flicked his hand towards her groin.

'Clean it,' he said.

'There was no way I was going to start pouring Dettol all over myself,' she said. 'I said no, and he looked cross. He started shouting and screamed at me to get undressed. I don't know why I did it, but I got undressed. I think I was more scared of what he'd do if I ignored him. I suppose I wasn't thinking straight. It was all so frightening.'

Once Carol was naked, Fayed instructed her to lie on the bed. 'He was fiddling with himself, getting himself aroused. It was vile – this wrinkly old man playing with himself to get an erection while I lay there. He was huffing and puffing and grunting and groaning, so I shut my eyes and tried not to think about it all. I was conscious that he was still playing with himself and moaning away, then he suddenly got off. He couldn't get an erection. He shouted something at me that I didn't understand, like the whole thing was my fault.'

Carol got up and got dressed, and was told to go into the dining room. She walked in to see three men there, all of Middle Eastern origin. She'd never seen any of them before.

'Now choose,' said Fayed. 'Which man you will have sex with?'

Carol stood in silence, unable to speak.

'Choose, or I choose for you.'

'I don't want to,' she said. 'Please let me go.'

'You sleep with my brother,' he said, and one of the men stood up and pushed me back into the bedroom.

Mohamed stopped him and said, 'No – here – for us all to see.'

Carol said her legs were trembling and it was obvious she was terrified, so Mohamed's brother took her into the bedroom, held her down and raped her.

'I didn't put up much of a fight. I was too scared. When I looked up, Fayed was looking through the bedroom door at us. I was worried that he would want to have sex with me next, and what of the other men? Was I going to have to sleep with them too?'

Carol doesn't know what happened next. She thinks she passed out, and she woke up in the dining room. Everyone had left except for Mohamed, who came over when she woke up and said she was sacked because she had chosen his brother Salah over him.

18

HUNTERS AND HUNTED

THE EFFORTS TO CATCH HIM

'We realised we were dealing with Maxwell levels
of dodgy. Crumbling finances, lying, cheating,
treating women appallingly. We had to speak
out about it all.'

Ian Hislop, editor of *Private Eye*, on the magazine's
'Phoney Pharaoh' campaign to expose Fayed

The puzzle is not so much that characters like Fayed exist – of course they do. From the beginning of time, tyrannical leaders have always walked among us. What's alarming is that so many honourable people from both inside and outside the company knew about Fayed and what he was doing, and yet still did nothing.

Those who were employed at Harrods were bound by the constraints of loyalty to the chairman and the fear of losing their jobs. But what about those outside the work-force?

Journalists will stop at nothing to expose wrongdoing, but so many of them appeared to bite their tongues.

Allison Pearson, a writer who says she was aware of Fayed's crimes, wrote in the *Telegraph*, 'You might ask why I, and countless other journalists, failed to expose him when there were women prepared to tell their stories twenty-five years ago. Welcome to two-tier British justice; for the few, not the many. Libel actions in this country are potentially so expensive that you need deep pockets to defend one.' She adds, 'The media will hesitate to run stories about rich, influential people who can afford the best barristers unless the evidence appears to be cast-iron. And victims are likely to be scared and easily intimidated.'

What Pearson describes is a textbook example of what legal experts call SLAPPs (strategic lawsuits against public participation). These are legal actions designed not to right a genuine wrong, but to silence those who seek to tell an inconvenient truth. The wealthy and powerful deploy SLAPPs as weapons against journalists, whistleblowers and activists. They're designed solely to intimidate. The person sending the SLAPP – usually a wealthy individual – files a lawsuit against someone who has criticised them publicly. The claim itself typically has little chance of succeeding in court, but that's not the point. The real objective is to cripple the defendant's financial resources through protracted legal proceedings until they're forced to give up.

The devastating effectiveness of SLAPPs lies in the way they favour the rich. For a billionaire like Fayed, spending £500,000 on legal fees is just another cost of doing business. For a journalist, however, such costs can be ruinous, potentially leading to bankruptcy. Even when media organisations have insurance against libel claims, insurers often pressure them to settle rather than fight, regardless of how strong their case may be.

This means that newspapers are cautious about investigating powerful figures with litigious reputations (something that Fayed definitely had). Stories are killed in editorial meetings not because they lack merit or public interest, but because the financial risk of publishing them is deemed too great. The effect of this is that the powerful become effectively untouchable. Joe Powell, the MP for Kensington and Bayswater, the constituency in which Harrods is located, said, 'They [SLAPPs] don't just protect reputations, they shield individuals from accountability and allow abuse to continue unchecked. And Al-Fayed died before he could face justice. But imagine how many women's lives would not have been ruined if anti-SLAPP legislation had been in place, and journalists had been able to report freely on the case.

'As far back as 1995, *Vanity Fair* published an article about Al-Fayed which detailed how he had sued the *Observer* over a story about the sources of his wealth. Other journalists were also threatened or sued. The journalist Maureen Orth wrote at the time that all critical reporting outside the *Observer* virtually stopped, and allegations of sexual abuse in the press were suppressed. In 2008 the *Mail on Sunday* prepared a report stating that Fayed was under investigation for sexually assaulting a fifteen-year-old. Legal threats forced them to remove his name, referring instead to a senior Harrods executive, and that is how SLAPPs work.'

The *Mail on Sunday* article Powell is referring to was written by Martin Smith, then the paper's crime correspondent. Smith discovered that Fayed was under investigation for sexually assaulting a fifteen-year-old, but the paper was unable to name him after receiving legal letters from Fayed's lawyers.

In the end they were forced to describe Fayed as a 'senior Harrods executive'. This was despite the Metropolitan Police, unusually, confirming that Fayed was the suspect. The Crown Prosecution Service did not prosecute the case on the grounds that the victim had been confused about the date on which she said she'd been attacked, meaning that the story disappeared. It went from being an incredible exclusive for Smith – a story with the power to expose Fayed and change history – to a non-story in which Fayed was never named and the police never prosecuted.

Chris Blackhurst, former editor of the *Independent* newspaper, admitted that he was not as harsh on Fayed as he should have been. 'We knew as well that he pursued young women relentlessly in his store,' he wrote in the *Evening Standard*, 'that they accused him of sexual assault. But we did nothing. It is only in death that we feel able to say much of this. When he was alive, I did not take him apart. I was as guilty as the next journalist who indulged his fantasies. Why? Because we were scared. The likelihood of litigation was real, he frequently sued those he took against, and he and his acolytes were not afraid to refer to the possibility of him doing so again. Proprietors and editors did not want to go there – life was too short, there was a paper to produce, a schedule to fill.'

Britain's draconian libel laws stifled forthright reporting, allowing him to operate with impunity, his activities

shielded from public scrutiny. Several noteworthy excep-
tions, however, stood fast against the tide.

Private Eye displayed remarkable courage, provoking
Fayed's wrath by dubbing him the 'Phoney Pharaoh'.
Vanity Fair, led by Henry Porter, broke ranks with a pene-
trating exposé by Maureen Orth; Tom Bower followed
this by crafting an unsparing biography in 1998 that laid
bare uncomfortable truths; and in 2017, Channel 4 broadcast *Al-Fayed: Behind Closed Doors.*

Then came the BBC documentary *Al Fayed: Predator at
Harrods* in 2024, which lifted the lid off a boiling caul-
dron. The genesis of the documentary is a fascinating tale
in its own right, and a huge tribute to one man's determination to right the wrongs of the past. Keaton Stone was a
self-financed journalist who worked for six years before
contacting the BBC with the evidence that would end up
in a huge, impactful documentary that we'll look at in
detail below.

But there were others. The *Evening Standard*, which
published an exposé that was entirely accurate, were
punished by Fayed. Overnight, he withdrew Harrods's
annual £1 million advertising campaign in the newspaper.
Arousing Fayed's anger was an expensive business.

The first publication to begin a campaign of revelations
about Fayed was *Private Eye* magazine, which started its
investigations into Fayed in 1984, a year before he bought
Harrods and long before the accusations of sexual misconduct began to leak out. The sobriquet 'Phoney Pharaoh'
was first used in early 1989 in the magazine's Slicker's

column ('In the City'), and the *Eye* continued, relentlessly and gloriously, for years with its usage of the name. This angered Fayed a great deal, which delighted Ian Hislop, the editor of the magazine since 1986, and his predecessor Richard Ingrams. 'Fayed wrote to me regularly,' says Hislop, 'complaining about us. It didn't bother me in the least; I knew we were getting somewhere.'

I meet Hislop at a *Private Eye* lunch in Soho to discuss the magazine's early pieces about Fayed. (If only all interviews I undertook for my investigation had been conducted in such convivial surroundings . . . On one occasion I met a Harrods security guard in his car in a car park because he was so paranoid about being seen with a journalist. On another, the woman I was meeting closed her curtains and requested we sit on the floor just in case people could see in through the gaps. Fayed may have died, but the fear lingers.)

Private Eye was dubious about Fayed from the start, thanks to 'Slicker', the influential investigative journalist whose column exposes corporate misconduct, accounting irregularities and City scandals. The column has built a reputation for being the first to identify troubling business stories, including Robert Maxwell's pension fund theft and the 2008 financial crisis, and so it was with Fayed.

'Slicker is very good at spotting which foreign businessmen have turned up and what they're after,' says Hislop. 'When the war broke out between Fayed and Tiny Rowland over the purchase of Harrods, we started covering it every issue in the City pages. We started asking: what on earth is this about? We knew he had connections to Papa Doc Duvalier, he'd bought the Ritz, he'd bought Harrods and was trying to buy the *Observer*. There was an extraordinary feeling of, who are you and what are you up to?'

No one understood where his money came from, no one understood anything about the man. The man was born to feed the City pages. Next he was trying to involve himself with the royal family. And you just thought, there's no part of British life that he does not want to put himself in the middle of. There were lots of stories of him scamming people, doing whatever was necessary to make money, behaving appallingly to women in his employ.

'He wanted everything. He wanted the castle in Scotland, to own *Punch* magazine, to own Harrods, to be a friend of the Queen. You know, he literally wanted to be at the heart of everything that foreigners imagine Britain is.

'As a journalist, you think: are you a suitable person to be at the heart of all our major institutions? I think not. And what do you want? You must want something out of this. Which he did. He wanted influence, money, status, acceptance – all of those things.'

As the Fayed story grew, it began its journey out of the City pages into the main body of *Private Eye*, and there it would stay. Fayed featured in the magazine – knocked and ridiculed by satirical pens – until his death.

'I looked in our index before I spoke to you,' says Hislop. 'And I mean, there are about fifty pages of articles about Fayed with ten entries to start off with – hundreds of stories. It's in more or less every issue. I suppose you could say we got quite obsessed, but there was a strong feeling that he was up to no good, and he was in the middle of everything. The more people we talked to, the more it seemed to be the case that Fayed was not what he claimed to be.

'We realised we were dealing with Maxwell levels of dodgy. Crumbling finances, lying, cheating, treating women appallingly. We had to speak out about it all. We didn't have any bent coppers who could come and arrest us for shoplifting when we'd done no such thing. He couldn't intimidate us because we didn't work for him.'

Fayed tried, though. He reacted to *Private Eye*'s coverage in his customary understated way. He bought *Punch* magazine and dedicated the entire first and second issues to trashing Hislop. 'There was a picture of my wife and me on the first page with her saying, "I'm going to leave you soon, because you're losing all your money." That was nice, you know? I mean, it wasn't even very funny.'

Fayed tried everything to get back at *Private Eye* but he never sued. Not once. 'We got endless abuse from him through any outlet he could find, but not legal. He never attempted to give me any brown envelopes either.' The magazine wrote hundreds, if not thousands, of articles about Fayed, all of them either revealing dreadful truths about him or mocking him, but even this most litigious of men never threw lawyers at this particular problem. The reason was because there was no legal case to answer. *Private Eye* was revealing the truth about Fayed. It was all entirely accurate.

The frustration was that no other publications picked up the story and ran with it, and the journalists at *Private Eye* were dismissed as being racist or snobbish. Fayed intimated that the reason for their opposition to him was because of the colour of his skin and the place of his birth. This was plainly nonsense, but it's a line he rolled out whenever anyone criticised him. This strategy of deflection – claiming that legitimate criticism stems from prejudice rather than facts – is a classic example of 'poisoning the well'. By reframing valid concerns as expressions of racism or class-based snobbery, Fayed attempted to undermine his critics' credibility and moral standing. Rather than addressing the substantive allegations against him, he sought to position himself as a victim of xenophobia, thereby shifting the conversation away from his actions and onto the supposed biases of his accusers.

But *Private Eye* was made of stronger stuff, and the stories kept coming.

While *Private Eye* battled away, attacking Fayed with a regularity which infuriated him, *Vanity Fair* were planning their own exposé.

In September 1995 the writer Maureen Orth wrote a searing piece about Fayed that sent everyone close to him spinning on their axes. The incredible article, full of accurate revelations about his behaviour, resulted in a legal battle between Fayed and Condé Nast, the owners of *Vanity Fair*, which continued until 1997, when the death of Fayed's son Dodi in Paris persuaded Condé Nast to call off the fight.

Looking at the *Vanity Fair* piece today is quite remarkable. Nearly two decades before the BBC documentary finally exposed him to the world, Orth highlighted the racist and sexist abuse, the sexual attacks, the trumped-up shoplifting charges, and the heavy use of recording devices and cameras around the public areas of the store and in the corporate offices. It cut to the core of what Fayed's organisation was all about, and it was excruciating for him. He threw all his legal might behind seeking retribution. Condé Nast brought the distinguished lawyer David Hooper on board to work alongside Henry Porter, *Vanity Fair*'s UK editor, to shore up their case.

Telling the story of the battle between *Vanity Fair* and Fayed is like wandering into a surreal gangster movie. Fayed was determined to win the fight against the magazine at any cost, so he reduced himself to the tactics of a thug. At one stage he asked Paul Handley-Greaves, a Harrods security officer, to approach Porter and offer to sell him a stolen, compromising video of Fayed. He figured that if Porter fell for it and bought the video, he could inform the police that Porter had bought stolen goods. Brilliant plan! Except for the minor fact that the video was non-existent, and Porter and Hooper saw through the scam straight away.

This transparent entrapment scheme was embarrassingly amateur for someone of Fayed's resources and position. As soon as the six-foot-six Handley-Greaves came through the door, Porter knew something was up. He said, 'Evidence like that doesn't fall into your lap.'

Their refusal to deal with Handley-Greaves should have been the end of it, but they later discovered Fayed's team had reported them to the City of London Police for attempting to purchase 'stolen property'. This was a bizarre accusation for two reasons: first, they'd point-blank refused to buy the video, realising immediately that it was a trap, and second, the video never existed in the first place. Dealing with Fayed was proving to be like nothing they'd ever experienced before.

There were frequent meetings between Fayed's team and the team at Condé Nast, including one when Michael Cole, Fayed's director of public affairs, attempted to negotiate with Nicholas Coleridge, head of Condé Nast in the UK. So concerned was Cole about the prospect of Coleridge turning up wearing a recording device that he insisted they met in a Turkish bath.

Vanity Fair did enjoy a huge stroke of luck, however, when Bob Loftus, a former police officer turned security director at Harrods, was dismissed by Fayed after the two fell out. Loftus chose to speak to Porter and Hooper about life at Harrods, rather than take Fayed's offer of a financial payout to keep quiet. The information that Loftus provided was incredible. It revealed the extent of the racism and sexual harassment that had taken place in the store, as well as all the spying on and recording of staff.

Loftus's witness statement was over fifty pages long and offered the world the most thorough account yet of what had been happening behind the scenes in Knightsbridge. Significantly, it confirmed that everything in Orth's article was accurate. *Vanity Fair* was getting somewhere.

Fayed's intimidatory tactics hadn't worked, and this detailed report from Loftus confirmed the details of their exposé. But just as all seemed to be going well for the magazine, along came the crash in the Pont de l'Alma Tunnel that claimed the lives of Fayed's son and Diana, Princess of Wales. The world sunk into a state of universal mourning, and Condé Nast, out of respect for Fayed's loss, shut the case down.

'Both sides absorbed their own costs, no damages were paid, and we agreed to place all evidence in locked storage. It seemed the right and humane decision in the immediate aftermath of the shocking deaths,' said Porter. 'But it wasn't, because of the countless women who have suffered since our case was settled, including many who were raped by a man who appeared unaffected by grief or regret.

'I argued we should act like a publication, not a business, and write another story revealing what we had discovered, but there was understandably no appetite to return to the subject of Mohamed Al Fayed.'

Maureen Orth's article, 'Holy War at Harrods', remains freely accessible online, a testament to journalistic persistence against extraordinary intimidation.

Four women on ITV's *The Big Story* – in a programme entitled 'Sex, Lies and Audiotape' – alleged in 1997 that they were repeatedly groped, subjected to crude remarks and promised rewards in return for sex. Fayed reacted angrily to the allegations and issued a statement condemning the claims as outrageous and untrue, arguing that they were a repetition of allegations previously made in the *Vanity Fair* article by disgruntled former employees.

A year after the death of Dodi, the investigative journalist Tom Bower wrote an 'unauthorised' biography of Fayed. His book was a coruscating take-down, detailing accusation after accusation and fact after fact that revealed the chairman of Harrods was utterly corrupt. The response from Fayed, you'll be unsurprised to hear, was as sophisticated as the man himself. He threatened to break Bower's fingers while he was in the process of writing the book so that he'd be unable to type it.

But, despite Bower's book exposing Fayed for what he was, nothing happened. There were no police investigations, no boycotting of Harrods, no withdrawals of invitations for Fayed. He'd been completely exposed, but life carried on the same. And so it was too with newspapers such as *The Sunday Times* and the *Mail on Sunday*, both of whose reporting of Fayed's misconduct was punchy and accurate but failed to stop Fayed in his tracks.

In 2017 Channel 4's *Dispatches* programme broadcast allegations of groping, assault and harassment, airing another investigation on *Channel 4 News* the following year. But even when he died, much of the media continued to broadcast and print bunkum praise about his august career, his generous charitable contributions, and his doting loyalty to his family.

* * *

Then, in 2024, *Al Fayed: Predator at Harrods* aired on the BBC, and the whole story was blown wide open. What had for decades remained whispered allegations and buried secrets was suddenly exposed to millions of viewers across Britain. The documentary landed with seismic force in a cultural landscape already transformed by a series of revelations about powerful men and their abuses.

The timing proved crucial. The programme emerged in the wake of the #MeToo movement, which had fundamentally altered how society responded to allegations of sexual misconduct. No longer were victims automatically doubted or dismissed; their stories now commanded attention and demanded action. The public had been educated, sensitised and mobilised by years of painful revelations.

Fayed's case struck viewers as particularly egregious, coming as it did after a succession of high-profile predators had been exposed: Harvey Weinstein in the movie business, Jeffrey Epstein in corporate America and Jimmy Savile within the BBC itself. Audiences had developed an understanding of how powerful men could weaponise their wealth and influence to abuse and ensure silence afterwards. Fayed's methods – the grooming, the isolation, the threats, the cover-ups – followed a playbook that had become distressingly familiar.

Yet the documentary still shocked the nation. Here was a man who had positioned himself at the heart of British high society, who had owned one of the country's most iconic institutions, who had cultivated relationships with royalty and politicians alike – all while allegedly perpetrating horrific abuses against vulnerable young women under his employment. The contrast between Harrods's glittering facade and the darkness that apparently lurked within its walls proved impossible to ignore.

Within hours of the broadcast, social media exploded with reactions. Within days, new victims came forward. Within weeks, there were calls for formal investigations, compensation schemes and wholesale reforms to employment protections. A story decades in the making had finally broken through.

The documentary began when the documentary maker Keaton Stone was helping his girlfriend Sophia – now his wife – with her CV. He re-jigged the document to put her role as a personal assistant to Fayed at the top, feeling that Harrods was a prestigious store and her role there should be highlighted. He expected her to be delighted with the changes he'd made. But she wasn't.

'She broke down crying, shaking,' Stone recalls. '"Why have you got his name on there?" she said. "Get him off, get him off." It was a horrible, visceral, upset and distraught reaction.'

What Stone didn't realise was that he'd unknowingly tapped into a deep and dark secret. At just twenty years old, Sophia had been the target of Fayed's persistent and repeated sexual assaults after he'd spotted her working on the shop floor at Harrods. Despite the fact that she had no relevant experience, he promoted her to be one of his personal assistants.

Sophia then explained to her boyfriend that Fayed had tried to rape her several times between 1988 and 1991. It began with uncomfortable 'cuddles' and attempts to kiss her, quickly escalating to 'grabbing and groping and hands everywhere up my skirt and down my top'. His vulgarity was a constant feature of his behaviour towards her, with Fayed saying things like 'give me some milk from your titties'. This harassment eventually escalated to four attempted rapes over three years – once at his Park Lane offices, twice in France, and, most traumatically, in his castle in Scotland, where Sophia finally fought back, 'screaming her head off and kicking him' until he gave up.

As a successful writer and documentary producer, Keaton Stone knew immediately that he'd found his next subject, and he worked for the next six years to gather all the explosive material for the documentary. 'I never set out to make a documentary, despite my job,' he says. 'It was purely deeply personal and something that had immensely upset me since I first heard from Sophia what happened to her. She really is the most gentle and kind soul, and so this was something I couldn't just let go.'

Sophia's anguished revelation shocked and angered her boyfriend. 'It was a love story, really,' he told Channel Nine's *60 Minutes* programme, 'and that thought of someone doing something horrendous, horrible to her . . . it absolutely broke me as well, broke my heart. I wanted to find out where it went, who it led to, who was involved.'

* * *

Keaton set himself up in the spare room, and later in a garden office, to piece the story together. He spoke to hundreds of people and amassed a pile of evidence that he took to the BBC in 2023, just before Fayed died, aiming to expose him and hold him to account while he was still alive. 'We desperately didn't want another [Jimmy] Savile situation,' he says. 'We wanted him in jail. How big it was meant that it took as long as it did, and sadly he did die, but it's still of overwhelming importance to the survivors that the world knows the truth about him.'

Stone's hunt for the truth uncovered so much more than he expected – what he describes as 'the world's worst case of corporate sexual abuse'. The scale was colossal, as victims in the US, Canada, Africa, Asia and Australia told their appalling stories. 'The horrors went all around the world,' says Stone. The BBC realised immediately how powerful his work was, describing it as 'absolutely extraordinary', with the head of documentaries calling it 'seismic'.

The impact of the documentary was immediate and far-reaching. Within days of its broadcast, hundreds of additional victims came forward, stretching support services beyond their limits. The Metropolitan Police, faced with mounting public pressure, announced a formal investigation into the institutional failures that had allowed Fayed's abuse to continue unchecked for decades, with former Harrods executives finding themselves facing uncomfortable questions about their knowledge and potential complicity. The documentary also sparked parliamentary debates about strengthening laws against SLAPPs and improving protections for whistleblowers in cases involving powerful figures.

There's no question that the documentary changed everything for Fayed's victims everywhere, and another documentary is coming soon, this one on Channel 5 by Little Gem, the same team that made the eviscerating programme about the Post Office scandal. And Stone continues to investigate. 'The story is far from over,' Stone says. 'It will only be over once the whole horror story is exposed and all those complicit are held to account, which is my focus now.'

19
THE PSYCHOPATH
BEHIND THE CHARM

'I'm building a glass pyramid over the Egyptian escalator where my body will be mummified, so my customers can come and see me forever.'

Fayed

It's a colourful word, loaded with terrifying suggestions of murder, evil and tyrannical behaviour. Every decent psychological thriller has one, and it's always the person you least expect . . . lurking in plain sight, destroying lives, and causing terror and misery wherever he or she goes: the psychopath.

This word has been liberally used to describe Fayed since he died, this apparently friendly man with a mischievous grin and twinkly eyes peering out from beneath his wild eyebrows. But was he a psychopath, what does the word actually mean and what are the criteria used to determine precisely who is one?

Professor Essi Viding is one of the world's leading experts in psychopathy. She won the Royal Society Rosalind Franklin Award for her achievements in the field of experimental psychology, has also received the British Academy Wiley Prize in Psychology and the British Psychological Society Spearman Medal, and she's a Fellow of the British Academy and the Academy of Medical Sciences. So she knows a thing or two. In particular, she knows all about psychopaths.

The natural place to start seems to be to ask her the most pressing question: what precisely is a psychopath? 'People who don't feel empathy or guilt,' she says. 'Those who can be superficially charming, have a grandiose sense of self-worth, manipulate other people and lie pathologically. They have an inability to feel with fellow human beings. They don't get their kicks out of affiliation and being close to other people. They might get their kicks out of dominating and putting other people down. Looking after number one is a key trait – "I am the only person who matters. My needs are the only needs that matter."'

Professor Viding does not want to be tempted into making psychological assessments of someone she's never met, and emphasises that she's not a clinical psychologist. This means that we're simply left with the evidence of his behaviour to assess whether Fayed possessed the traits that fit her descriptions of a psychopath. One of the traits that stands out in her definition is 'a grandiose sense of self-worth'.

One is drawn to this statement of Fayed's when asked about his death: 'I'm building a glass pyramid over the Egyptian escalator where my body will be mummified, so my customers can come and see me forever. Have you seen the Egyptian escalator? You have my face on four figures on every floor. The Egyptian room, which is like a mini "Temple of Karnak". You have twelve sphinxes. I put my face on each. It's a listed monument, so they can't take me away, they can't.'

Another of Viding's descriptions of psychopaths – 'They might get their kicks out of dominating and putting other people down' – chimes with the story told by Philippa about Fayed laughing when a woman started crying after he forced her to crawl on the floor and pretend to be a donkey. He laughed even more when some of the other women began crying too. His delight in the pain and humiliation of others was there for all to see, as it was when Suzanne said he laughed after attacking her.

Researchers have spent decades trying to establish why some people are like this and others aren't. Omar, Fayed's third and youngest son, has on numerous occasions expressed his conviction that his father's attitudes to life in general, and women in particular, arose as a result of his losing his mother when he was young: 'He lost his mother at the age of seven and didn't have any stable female figure in his life growing up,' he says. 'We all know how impactful that can be to a child's psychological development. That was really one of the most fundamental things. The way that he spoke with women, to women, about women was entirely the result of growing up without a mother.'

Viding is not convinced by this argument. 'There are a lot of people who lose a mother when they're young,' she counters, 'but very few turn out like him. That's not to say that it will not have had any impact on him. I think it would be hard to imagine a young child losing his mother and it not affecting him, but I think it would be totally implausible to say that that is the sole cause of him being the way he was. There are so many people who lose their mothers at that age and who do not turn out that way. Losing a mother doesn't turn you into a psychopath or a sadistic bully.

'So there must be something else there in the mix. For someone to grow up uncaring, bullying and manipulative, there are likely to be genetic factors that predispose to this kind of behaviour, and often other life experiences.'

'So, what does determine who becomes a psychopath?' I ask. 'Is it nature or is it nurture?'

'Well, both. The easiest way to think of it is that nature provides a window within which you will function, but exactly where you are within that window, or continuum, is shaped by your environment, opportunities and choices. So it's not inevitable that someone with particular genes will end up a psychopath or a sadist, but if you have a constellation of risk genes, you will be more likely to turn out that way.

'Think about physical attributes – athleticism, for instance. I don't think anyone has difficulty in accepting that there are big genetic differences between individuals that influence whether someone is likely to become a top athlete in a particular sport or not. The kind of genetically influenced biological attributes that make you a good shot-putter are very different from those that make you a good long-distance runner. A shot-putter could improve their time on a ten-kilometre run, and a long-distance runner could increase their shot-put result, but not to the degree that the person who has a biological predisposition to be a top athlete in either sport could.

'If the roll of the genetic dice predisposes you to develop psychopathy, you might develop to be very mean and very unempathetic and very calculated and nasty to people. But there's no question that you can be socialised in a way that makes you think, actually, it's better for me to look after number one in ways that don't put other people down and don't hurt other people.

'Like the shot-putter that tries long-distance running, a person who has a genetic risk to develop psychopathy is unlikely to be the most naturally empathetic person on the planet, but they may be socialised in a way that means they do not hurt others and allows them to at least feign interest in other people's well-being. So they might be perfectly nicely socialised and be perfectly law-abiding, and even thrive in certain careers where you have to be quite bold and unemotional. But no one with that roll of the genetic dice is going to be the next Oprah.'

Some studies have shown clear differences in brain function between psychopaths and non-psychopaths. Scientists have demonstrated that the neural circuitry involved in emotion, empathic and reward processing is compromised in those with elevated risk of developing psychopathy. Studies also show that those brain areas that mediate fear, guilt, joy and empathy – including the amygdala and the insular cortex – are underactive in psychopathy, and that the areas associated with impulsivity, aggression, sensation and risk-taking, including the orbitofrontal cortex and striatum, are not working as they should. So the traits are shown clearly in the measurable reactions of the brain to stimuli.

Other research has been conducted to look at children's brains when reacting to photographs of people in painful situations. Among children with the highest levels of callous and unemotional traits there was the lowest reaction to seeing people in pain. What researchers have shown is that children who are at risk of developing psychopathy resonate less with other people's distress and don't seem to experience positive emotions in the same way. Again, their brains appear predisposed to working in a certain way.

Extreme psychopathic traits, however, are not at all common. It's estimated that only 1 per cent of the population have clinically problematic levels of callous and unemotional traits, but this percentage rises in the corporate world, where it's estimated that the figure could be as high as 3 per cent and often affecting those in positions of power.

A paper in the September 2024 issue of the *Journal of Economic Criminology*, in a very similar definition to the one proposed by Viding, characterises corporate psychopaths as being:

> superficially charming, with a grandiose sense of
> self-worth. They are people with low personal
> integrity; pathological liars who are good at conning
> and manipulating, have no remorse about harming
> others, and are emotionally shallow, calculating,

callous and lacking in empathy and further, that they are people who fail to take responsibility for their own actions.

Researchers suspect that there's a greater proportion of psychopaths in the business world than in the general population because succeeding in business involves being aggressive and beating others, meaning that anti-social behaviours are often ignored on the assumption that the person is simply behaving in a 'businesslike way'.

According to an academic paper by Sheehy, Boddy and Murphy into corporate psychopaths:

Research in the United Kingdom among a tightly defined sample of managers, for example, found that 35 per cent of all workplace bullying was associated with the presence of psychopathic leaders.

Similarly, a sample of managers in Australia concluded that around 26 per cent of all bullying is accounted for by 1 per cent of the employee population, and it would appear that in many cases, the bullies are corporate psychopaths.

Christine Pratt is CEO of the National Bullying Helpline. She says:

The motivating factors for bullying are: ego and blinkered, biased, self-importance, and a view that they are above the law and/or untouchable. Bullies are often narcissists who are egotistical and frequently delusional. Some may not even realise that they are controlling others. The narcissist may not accept that they are narcissistic in any way. The traits and characteristics can stem from personal traumas and/or experiences and a deep-rooted mental attitude, dominated and led by differing circumstances. Fayed may have had resentment issues or issues linked to his upbringing or even culture. He wanted to rule the world. He wanted to control our royal family through Diana – it seems.

A lot of these behaviours reflect a craving for power and control, and some might even be mental-health-related. 'Certainly, the mindsets in every case are out of touch with reality,' says Pratt. 'They are in a perverse world of their own.'

One of the hardest things to understand about Fayed is the joy he seemed to derive from others' misery. It might be that we all cause sadness or pain to others on occasion, but surely it is something that most people subsequently deeply regret. In the course of my research, talking to dozens of people who were abused by Fayed or had negative experiences with him, not a single person said that he ever apologised or showed any remorse. They say, instead, that he revelled in their pain and misery, acting as if he'd done nothing wrong, or was entitled, in some way, to behave as he did.

According to Viding, 'This is not, diagnostically, a core characteristic. You may have individuals who have high levels of psychopathy and who don't seek to humiliate someone else for kicks. However, if feeling powerful and dominant is something that brings you pleasure, then not having empathy and not feeling guilt are going to be very, very helpful for you in that context.

'In a way, it's hard to imagine how someone could systematically bully and humiliate others, if they actually had genuine empathy. If you have empathy for others, you will obviously care about their needs, not just your own. If you have no empathy, then the only person who really matters is you and what you want.'

A number of key questions remain. What can be done about these people? Can we identify them and protect society from them before they cause harm to others? It's not such an easy thing to do.

'It's unrealistic to think that you're ever going to weed all of these individuals out of society,' says Viding. 'In order to reduce their impact, we need to think about prevention, and, failing that, treatment or incarceration. But not everyone wants to be treated or will be caught for their bad behaviour. This means that we also need to better understand how we can protect people.

'We need more research on victims. Why do some people fall prey to being victimised, perhaps more easily than others? What can we do to help those people who may be more vulnerable to help them spot the kinds of things that are danger signs. We know from decades of research that it's not random who gets bullied and victim- ised by psychopaths. These guys can sniff out who's easy to victimise. They don't indiscriminately go after everybody, and that's absolutely not to victim-blame. Just because you may be vulnerable, that doesn't mean that you're fair game, but what it does mean is that we need to get better at helping people who might be more vulnerable.

'And we also need, obviously, workplace cultures and systems in place to protect people and ensure that bad behaviour is not tolerated. It should not just be left to individuals to spot the signs and even if they manage to do that, there may not always be a way to protect yourself.'

To an overwhelming extent, Fayed got away with his behaviour during his lifetime. There were journalists and media organisations in pursuit of him, and the police spoke to him on a couple of occasions, but nothing stopped him. Nothing happened that alerted the wider public to his behaviour. His riches enabled him to buy people off and surround himself with lawyers. He was known to be highly litigious, and this stopped many newspapers from pursuing him.

There's something quite hideous about the fact that his wealth, accumulated illegally and immorally, was used to further his illegal and immoral behaviour. The very same money he'd scammed and stolen from others was employed to buy his way out of any trouble.

This is something that instantly resonates with Viding. 'If you're rich and powerful, you're more likely to get away with things. There's something very disturbing about this. If you lack conscience and shame for your behaviour, you don't feel guilty, you continue to feel entitled. The money you have buffers you from facing the consequences of your behaviour within the justice system.

'There's an extensive literature about individuals with high levels of psychopathic features manipulating, lying, cheating and acquiring wealth by dishonest means and exploiting people with the money they have. This dishonesty and wiliness to con and exploit others is one of the characteristics of psychopathy.'

One of the big problems with psychopaths is identifying and then avoiding them. When they're in full bloom, behaving recklessly and harmfully, it's easy to spot them, but they wear a shield of superficial charm and kindness that protects them.

Although Viding is extremely knowledgeable about psychopaths, she says that even after a lifetime of studying them, she'd struggle to identify one from just a single meeting. I ask her whether, if I sat twelve people in front of her, one of whom was a psychopath, and asked her to pick him or her out after a brief chat to each of them, would she be able to?

'No, not at all. I remember interviewing someone in prison a very long time ago, who was incredibly charming. I did all the interviews blind, so I'd no idea what his status was. He was telling me all about how he had a son, and he'd worked in a business, and he wanted to leave the business to the son. He said that it was breaking his heart that he was in a prison and couldn't be there for his son. I really felt for him. We did the whole interview, then I went to his file to read it through. He had five kids with four different women, none of whom he'd ever looked after. I was utterly sold in the interview. I believed him.

'One of the key things I've come to realise is that if you look at a person's file and then at what they say – if they're very different – you might have a problem. If what they say bears no resemblance to reality, there's a pretty good chance that something is seriously amiss. The critical thing to remember about psychopaths is that they care only about themselves. No one else's feelings concern them.

'Social psychologists have coined the term "ingroup". These are people that we're close to who are important to us. It's almost as if individuals with psychopathy have an ingroup that consists of one person, themselves. Anything and anyone else are dispensable.'

Whether or not we choose to define Fayed as a psycho-path – and it would be a brave person who'd refuse to do so – there's no question that he possessed many of the key traits that form the definition of psychopathy. There's also no question that, because of this, he was difficult to see for who he really was. People trusted him until it was too late. It meant that he was free to continue finding victims, and continue attacking women who trusted him, because he was the chairman and he seemed so friendly.

20

THE FAMILY DYNASTY

'I always got dirty old man vibes from my father.'

Omar Fayed

JAYNE

It's a cool, bright morning, and I'm with a group of people at a table in a bustling café in the shadow of Hampton Court Palace. It's a convivial gathering, with everyone chatting and drinking coffee. The conversation canters through many subjects and eventually turns to Fayed. A look of horror flits across the faces of everyone present. They've all heard the stories, and no one can quite believe what he did.

Then Jayne speaks. 'I worked at Harrods,' she says. Everyone turns to look at her. My heart sinks. She's incredibly beautiful – slim and leggy, with delicate features. She's exactly Fayed's type, and with her well-honed English accent would appeal to him immensely. I fear this is where the conversation will slide inexorably into pain and horror. But no, for here's a story with a difference, one with a positive twist. There's a good guy in this tale, and that's vanishingly rare regarding anything to do with Mohamed Fayed.

Jayne worked at Harrods in her late teens during the summer holidays in the mid-2000s. She was based in the personal shopping department for two summers, then, when work dried up there, Fayed extended a personal invitation to her to work in his office at the top of the building.

'One of his staff looked after me and set me up on the system. I was called an "office assistant", but in reality I did lots of things,' she explains. 'I had to fill up a room with toys from the toy department for when his children came to play. The room was packed full of all the best toys in Harrods. The next minute I'd be answering phones. I did whatever was required. There were five women in the office, all blonde and attractive, in their twenties and thirties.'

Her early experiences of working with Fayed were similar to those of many other attractive women working at the store. He gave her money and told her to go and buy some clothes. 'He liked us to be dressed very corporately and not scruffily. He hated high heels – we could only wear flats.' She estimates that she was paid an extra £200 to £300 a week by Fayed in bundles of notes. 'It was a huge amount of money for someone that age. In return, he wanted hugs from me, which made me feel uncomfortable, so I'd pull away. I never thought it was just me – I saw him do it to other girls. Everyone looked uncomfortable when he did it, but no one said anything.'

She says the reason no one spoke about the unwelcome physical contact was the awareness that everything they said and did was being recorded. 'I mentioned the unwelcome hugs on the escalator one day when I was travelling out of the store with one of the other women from the office, but she quashed the conversation very quickly. No one wanted to say anything negative because they knew – no matter where you said it – news would get back to him.'

The bugging of every part of the women's store life acted as a way to keep female employees isolated, unable to communicate properly with one another and thus more beholden to him. 'His office was, as far as I'm aware, the only place in which recording didn't take place,' says Jayne.

During her time working for Fayed, he made her many offers: he told her she should become a buyer, and he would help her; he asked her whether she'd like to go to Paris; he told her she should come and see his offices in Park Lane; he suggested that she come to his apartment for a party.

Sensibly, she resisted all such overtures and tried her hardest to remain professional while keeping a safe distance. She admits to feeling scared at times. 'When you had a brief conversation with him, he came across as easy-going and sweet-natured, but there was a hard side to him, and everyone was in fear of him.'

It was in this atmosphere of quiet fear, where young women like Jayne navigated Fayed's inappropriate behaviour while trying to keep their jobs, that an unexpected moment of decency emerged. One day, when leaving the chairman's office, Fayed's youngest son Omar approached her and handed her a note. On it he'd written a stern warning, advising her never to be alone with his father because of the danger he posed.

It might not sound like much, but it was something. Omar was only nineteen at the time, and offering friendly help and advice that would surely have earned the wrath of his father was a brave and decent thing to do. In the context of what we now know about Fayed – the numerous allegations of sexual harassment, assault and abuse of power that have emerged – Omar's warning takes on a more significant meaning.

Bravery and decency are scarce commodities when it comes to understanding the Fayed family. Indeed, Omar is the only person in the family who acted to help, rather than hinder, and he's the only family member to have spoken out since his father's death. Following the extensive media coverage of all the numerous allegations, Omar moved quickly to say that his father had been a 'wonderful dad' but that this 'does not blind me from an objective assessment of circumstances. The extent and explicit nature of the allegations are shocking and has thrown into question the loving memory I had of him. How this matter could have been concealed for so long and in so many ways raises further disturbing questions. I firmly believe that anyone found guilty of such reprehensible actions, including having facilitated, enabled or helped cover up such actions, no matter their status, must be held accountable.'

Fayed's wife Heini Wathén, whom he married in 1985 and remained with until his death in 2023, has by contrast remained silent. Indeed, she wrote in a WhatsApp message to her son: 'Don't speak to the press.' Omar defied her, as he did his father previously. His brother Karim and sisters Jasmine and Camilla have also remained silent, out of public view and away from the cameras, so it has fallen to the youngest son to lead the conversation.

When he spoke to the *Mail on Sunday* he said he'd always got 'dirty old man vibes' from his father. This ties in with his note to Jayne, warning her not to be alone with him. Omar knew something was going on, but had no idea of the extent of it at the time. He was unaware of the depths of depravity to which his father had sunk, but he recognised that his father's relationship with women was troubled – 'I always put my father's chauvinist approach and manner towards women down to a generational and cultural thing. It all became so tiresome and clichéd.'

Omar says that he's a very different man to his father. While Fayed Senior was interested in business and the accumulation of wealth, prestige and power, Omar developed a passion for environmental causes, founding ESTEE (Earth Space Technical Ecosystem Enterprises). When Omar expressed no interest in taking over the family business it led to a divide between father and son, and their estrangement in the years before Fayed's death.

'We are different people. We want different things. I wanted to take risks and not be as money-orientated as my father,' says Omar. One might argue that wanting 'different things' and to 'take risks' are immeasurably easier with Daddy's millions to fall back on, but Omar's decision not to run the family business meant he was forced to endure a complex relationship with his father so he could pursue a life he felt comfortable with. He resigned from the Harrods board in 2009 because the store 'wasn't doing anything positive for the future of humanity'.

Another way in which Omar says he differs from his father is in his attitude to women. He has always favoured long-term, steady relationships. He said his father made fun of the fact that Omar only had long-term girlfriends and urged him to play the field. Similar advice came from his father's younger brother Salah, who died in 2010 and has posthumously been accused of several sexual assaults, rape, drugging and human trafficking. Omar says that Salah once told him that he should sleep around, but warned him, 'Don't dip your pen in the company ink.'

Following the death of their father, the Fayed children have been engaged in some high-profile battles. Much like *Succession*, the BAFTA-winning TV series in which a wealthy media owner's sons and daughter fight over the inheritance of their father's empire, Fayed's progeny have been locked in conflict. Omar was involved in a legal case against his sister Camilla and her husband Mohamad Esreb after claiming there was a 'physical altercation' with Esreb when Omar was ambushed during a meeting at their father's estate in Surrey. Omar sought £100,000 in damages and alleged this was part of a planned assault by Camilla and Esreb. They denied the allegations and countered that Omar was a drug user. Omar denied the claim, but his sister insisted it was true.

Omar has previously spoken about taking 'an unholy amount of magic mushrooms'. Indeed, he claimed that it had a profound impact on him: 'It was nothing short of terrifying, a horrific experience – my friend and I thought we had died. But it was a positive accident in retrospect. My whole brain was reset to ground zero and I had a moment where I realised how little I actually knew about what was going on.'

After that, Omar dabbled in philosophy, religion, the environment and even had a job as a trader in the City. He attempted several ventures, from producing documentaries on psychedelics for medical purposes to co-founding a CBD (cannabidiol) company before he developed a passion for environmental causes.

The power struggle he's been engaged in – against his mother, brother and sisters for control over his father's estate – has divided the family. Those close to the Fayed clan say that Omar's eagerness to take over the estate is out of kilter with both his position in the order of succession and his claims that he's not as money-orientated as his father. 'Why not walk away from it all, if he's so opposed to everything his father stood for?' asks a source within the Fayed circle. 'One minute he's saying that his father's wealth appals him – well, don't have it then. Next, he says that he thinks the way his father treated women and the disabled was awful, but he thinks he should inherit everything because he has sisters and a brother with a disability, so it should all be his.'

Omar was contacted for comment, but didn't respond to numerous calls and messages. He previously claimed that he was the victim of a 'sibling power struggle'.

It's not hard to see why there'd be friction between Fayed's offspring, with billions in the bank (he was estimated to be worth £1.7 billion when he died), luxury apartments in Mayfair and Manhattan, nine Rolls-Royces, an extensive fine art collection, a Surrey mansion with an estimated value of £100 milion and his Paris Ritz Hotel worth £500 million.

When telling the Fayed story, one of the most frequently asked questions is what did his wife think of it all? Why would a former model and renowned beauty, twenty-six years Fayed's junior, hang around with this ageing lothario and put up with the constant cheating?

Was it for money? But surely no money can compensate for the undignified, humiliating life she endured. Or was it to keep the family together? Perhaps she didn't know what he was up to? This seems implausible.

Wathén has been mocked for her relationship with Fayed, and described variously as 'a prisoner in golden chains' and 'a doormat for him to wipe his golden shoes on'. But the truth is that the psychological dynamics at play in such relationships are often complex. Women who stay with unfaithful or abusive partners frequently face a web of emotional, social and practical barriers to leaving: a combination of emotional dependency, fear of change, concern for the children and the gradual erosion of self-confidence that makes leaving seem impossible. For someone like Wathén, who'd built her entire adult life around Fayed, the prospect of walking away from that identity would have been daunting, regardless of financial considerations.

She once said: 'My job is to look after my four lovely children.' The eldest of these lovely children is Jasmine, a fashionista who dropped out of her degree at the London College of Fashion and set up a fashion label, half eponymous, half searingly self-aggrandising. Jasmine di Milo combined her name with that of the famous statue of Venus, or Aphrodite – the ancient goddess of love – found on the Greek island of Melos. Milo was also the nickname of her younger sister, Camilla. Despite the label being funded by her father and the clothes being for sale in his store, it didn't work out and the company folded in 2010. She has kept a low profile ever since with her partner, Noah Johnson, a Welsh boxing star, world disco-dancing champion and heavy-metal rocker.

Karim is the next child and the eldest living son. He is deaf, a result of contracting meningitis when he was a toddler. Today he's a businessman and photographer, and is married to Brenda Costa, a deaf Brazilian supermodel, businesswoman and former Olympic swimmer from Brazil who runs a modelling agency promoting diversity and inclusion in the fashion industry. Karim has shown no interest in joining the family firm, preferring to keep a low profile. Unlike Omar, who has been vocal in his criticism of his father, Karim has chosen a path of quiet dignity, focusing on his own endeavours and charitable work. When he was eleven he was sent away to board at the Mary Hare School for deaf children. 'The hardest thing was socialising, making new friends,' he said. 'At that point, in all my life I hadn't spent more than a week apart from my parents. It was hard to adapt, to build a new life. But slowly things came together, and the school gave me some very valuable skills.'

When he spoke to the *Evening Standard* in one of the few interviews he's given, Karim spoke about the difficulties of being part of the Fayed family. 'It's difficult, yes,' he said. 'It has certainly opened doors for me. But you have to be very careful who you mix with. I have always tried to treat people exactly the same regardless of their status in life but I have come across those who want to know me just because they think I have money.'

He opened the Karim Fayed Hearing Centre in 2009, where people with hearing loss can have free tests and get bespoke hearing aids made. 'Being deaf has not shaped me as a person,' Karim said. 'My development has nothing to do with being deaf. I am a positive person – otherwise this [the hearing centre] would never have come out.' He donates half of the profits every year to the Mary Hare School.

Camilla is the third eldest, and the most unconventional – a vegan socialite whose background is littered with small acts of rebellion, like attempting to run away from school and go to the pub with friends. She attended Roedean, the exclusive all-girls boarding school, leaving when she was sixteen, then did one term at drama school before joining Harrods, where she worked under her mother's maiden name to minimise attention.

She says that her time on the shop floor at Harrods gave her a huge love of fashion, so she took a job at British *Vogue* before moving to New York and becoming an assistant to Anna Wintour. She then persuaded her father to buy her the fashion brand Issa in 2011, and the following year she married Mohamad Esreb in a register office, with no family members present. She'd met the Syrian property tycoon in a nightclub years earlier.

'Camilla resembles her father in many ways, particularly in her stubbornness and determination,' says a family friend, 'yet she never discovered her true calling. Even in her youth, she seemed directionless, unsure of her path.'

This indecision is evident in her career trajectory. After developing a passion for fashion and receiving the fashion brand Issa as a gift, she sold the business in 2016. She then reinvented herself in the wellness industry, launching Notting Hill's Farmacy restaurant and relocating to a Kent farm.

Farmacy received mixed reviews. In the *Observer*, Marina O'Loughlin wrote: 'Despite being marketed as "healthy choice comfort foods", the offerings disappointed. The "sourdough" pizza had all the character of an inflated Ryvita, topped with bright vegan cheese that looked and smelled like burst boils. The burger was a dense mass of black fibre that lingered unpleasantly. The sweet potato fries were nice, though. And the trendy "Earth Bowls" were merely random ingredients thrown together for easy consumption – pure infantilism.' Farmacy closed its doors in 2024.

In May 2010, after twenty-five years of ownership and at eighty-one years of age, Fayed sold Harrods to Qatar Holding, the sovereign wealth fund of the Qatar Investment Authority, for £1.5 billion. In the official announcement, Lazard, Fayed's financial advisers confirmed the transaction, while Fayed stated that he wanted to 'retire and spend more time with his children and grandchildren'.

The deal came after several approaches from Qatar Holding over the years. Fayed had previously insisted that he would never sell Harrods, famously declaring that only "if somebody offered me £10 billion" would he consider parting with the store. However, the economic climate following the 2008 financial crisis altered the retail landscape significantly.

Ken Costa, chairman of Lazard International, who advised Fayed on the sale, told the press, 'After twenty-five years as chairman of Harrods, Mohamed Al-Fayed has decided to retire and to sell Harrods to Qatar Holding.' He added that it was a 'landmark transaction' and emphasized that Qatar Holding would be 'good for London'. Qatar Holding's chairman, Sheikh Hamad bin Jassim bin Jabr Al-Thani, who also served as Qatar's prime minister, described Harrods as a 'symbol of British luxury and elegance' and promised to 'build on its traditions'.

Following the sale, Fayed retained ownership of his other assets, including the Ritz Hotel in Paris and Fulham Football Club, though he would eventually sell the latter to Shahid Khan in 2013 for approximately £200 million.

Mohamed Fayed died on 30 August 2023 at his Surrey estate. He was ninety-four years old, and his death was attributed to old age and natural causes after a period of declining health. Since selling Harrods, Fayed largely retreated from public life and lived a relatively secluded existence at Barrow Green Court. He was cared for by his loyal wife, Heini Wathén. His health had declined significantly, and reports indicated he suffered from dementia in his later years, which progressively worsened, requiring round-the-clock care. Despite the numerous scandals and allegations of infidelity that had plagued their marriage, Wathén remained steadfastly by his side.

As the Fayed children move forward with their lives in the aftermath of their father's death and the shocking allegations against him, they face the complex challenge of reconciling their personal memories with his public legacy. Each has chosen a different path – Omar's environmental activism and outspokenness, Karim's quiet philanthropy, Jasmine's retreat from public life and Camilla's series of entrepreneurial ventures.

The shadow of their father looms large over all of them, a complicated inheritance that goes far beyond the billions in his estate. For these children, raised in extraordinary wealth but also extraordinary dysfunction, the true challenge may be finding their own identities separate from the man who dominated not only their lives but also the lives of countless employees who crossed his path.

And for women like Jayne, who encountered Fayed and survived relatively unscathed, there remains the unsettling knowledge that their experiences were part of a much larger pattern – one that was allowed to continue unchecked for decades while those who might have intervened remained silent.

CONCLUSION

LEGACY OF TRAUMA

HOPE FOR CHANGE

Belinda still has nightmares about the abortion she was forced to have after being raped by Fayed. It all happened years ago but the images feel as clear as they ever were, visions of her younger self walking down the roads near her home, the big security guards marching by her side.

The looks they gave her, as if she were responsible for her rapist's actions. Those glances burned into her, and she spent a long time thinking that perhaps she was responsible. Did she send him the wrong signals? How could she have behaved differently? Perhaps if she'd been stronger, she could have fought him off? Was this all her fault?

She doesn't think that now. She realises that Fayed is the guilty one, not her, but it doesn't make the pain of what she went through any easier. In fact, it makes it harder. It makes her feel more vulnerable that someone could have just taken her and broken her like that. She says it makes her not want to leave the house some days.

'If I'd done something wrong, I could have learned from it and made sure I never did that again, but when you do nothing wrong and go about your business – working hard and being good to people – and you still suffer the pain, humiliation and psychological damage that I went through, it's really tough. Then you know that you are truly vulnerable. I've spent my life feeling frightened because of what he did, and the consequences of that.'

She says there's always a moment every morning when she wakes up with a start and realises she's OK. She feels out for the mattress, the pillows, her duvet. She looks for the light coming in through her blinds, watching the way it settles in sunny stripes on the duvet, and her mind settles. She's not back there. She's not at Harrods any more. Those days are long behind her. Fayed is dead. The fear must go now.

But it doesn't. Never. It's always there, within her and all around her.

After the pain of the abortion had begun to fade, she realised she'd developed this habit of scratching at her skin as if wanting to tear it off. She says her hands are always red and bleeding. On the day I met her they were bleeding a lot, scabbed and raw. 'Most days I have to change the sheets when I wake up because of the blood on them,' she says. 'I'm worse when I'm asleep. That's when the memories are at their most powerful and I dig and dig at my skin with my fingernails. There's blood everywhere, there's skin beneath my nails, and there's blood all over the pillows and sheets.'

She knows she'll suffer from this for the rest of her life. She knows she'll dig her fingernails into the soft flesh of her hands forever. That way the pain inside becomes real, becoming a wound she can see and treat. The wound inside is different. She describes it as huge, invisible and all-consuming. She can't understand it and she can't control it.

This is what Fayed did. He laughed and joked, he schemed and lied, cheated and stole, abused and bullied, and he broke people like Belinda and tossed them aside.

Belinda's not afraid to say that she has contemplated suicide. She tried once but called for help before it was too late and was saved by a stay in hospital. They asked her about her hands while she was there, but she refused to talk about them. They offered her therapy, but she's too scared to go. She feels like her emotions are on a knife edge, and counselling would shake the knife and send her crashing to the ground.

She clings on to the fact she was about to commit suicide but chose not to. 'I chose to live,' she says, with a rare smile. 'I don't think there's much of me that isn't broken by him, but my spirit is still there, just . . .'

The simple facts now. At the risk of stating the obvious, this should never have happened and it must never happen again. Women like Belinda should have been protected from men like Mohamed Fayed. Not in a patronising, condescending way, but protected in the way that we all need protection from evil. He shouldn't have been anywhere near the position he was in. He shouldn't have got there and he certainly shouldn't have been allowed to remain there, but he thrust money, NDAs and gifts at anyone who caused him a problem, whether it was paying MPs to ask questions for him in the House of Commons, shoving £20 notes down the tops of teenage girls or organising trips to Paris for senior police officers. He paid people off, he ingratiated himself with people and he used his payments as sticks with which to beat them. If you took money from Fayed, you were complicit. He'd make sure everyone knew. His generosity was the first of his two greatest weapons.

The second was the fear he engendered in his staff. While he smiled at babies and gave toys to toddlers, he left others so crippled by anxiety and terrified of what he'd do next that they were barely able to function. In Harrods, he did this through the people he employed to assist him in his reign of terror. He brought in people who could act with impunity as long as they showed loyalty. He threw money at these people, brown envelopes tossed in the direction of security guards, young women, older PAs who ran his empire – anyone who'd help him. If they hadn't done his dirty work, Fayed wouldn't have been able to get away with it.

There were dozens, perhaps hundreds of people who knew what was going on, or had an idea that all was not well. Some fought back, but many of them found it hard to speak out. Perhaps the senior members of staff at Harrods felt safer looking the other way. I'm sure the security guards were genuinely fearful of Fayed, but can they listen to Belinda's story and still feel that what they did was right? Can they picture her screaming herself to sleep and waking up covered in blood and think, 'That's fine, it doesn't matter that I didn't say anything'? Can the serving police officers who took brown envelopes and trips to the Paris Ritz say in all conscience that what they did was fine? What of the people in middle management who heard the rumours and saw the letters? Can they read these stories and feel reasonably relaxed about what they did?

Could Fayed's crimes have been exposed before his death? Yes, they could have, but the uncomfortable truth is that before the #MeToo movement transformed our cultural landscape, most crimes like this went unreported. For those of his victims who did try to speak out, the odds were stacked heavily against them.

The #MeToo movement, which exploded into public consciousness in 2017 following the *New York Times*'s exposure of Harvey Weinstein's decades of abuse, fundamentally changed how society responds to allegations of sexual misconduct by powerful men. Before Weinstein's fall, there existed what can only be described as institutional protection for powerful abusers, a system that normalised predatory behaviour and silenced victims through intimidation, financial settlements and legal threats.

Like Weinstein, Fayed used his power and wealth to create a fortress around himself. But unlike Weinstein, Fayed enjoyed additional layers of protection. He commanded not just a business empire but cultivated relationships with the Metropolitan Police, developing such close ties that officers were essentially compromised. The system didn't just fail to protect his victims – it actively collaborated in their silencing.

What's particularly chilling is how Fayed deployed SLAPPs (strategic lawsuits against public participation), designed not to win cases but to intimidate and financially drain critics into silence. These weren't merely defensive measures; they were offensive weapons in his arsenal. He brandished the threat of ruinous litigation against anyone who dared to speak out, ensuring that newspapers, former employees and potential whistleblowers remained terrified into compliance. The astronomical costs of defending even a baseless lawsuit meant that truth itself became a luxury few could afford.

The reality of this is that stories were killed in editorial meetings not because they lacked merit or public interest, but because the financial risk of publishing them was deemed too great to bear. The effect of this was that the powerful became effectively untouchable.

This devastating combination – a pre-#MeToo culture of disbelief towards victims, compromised law enforcement and the threat of financial destruction through legal action – created what was essentially a perfect shield for Fayed's crimes. His victims found themselves not only traumatised but utterly alone, facing a system engineered to protect the powerful rather than the vulnerable.

The BBC documentary that eventually exposed Fayed's crimes the year after his death became the catalyst for a long-overdue reckoning. But what does justice look like when the primary perpetrator is beyond the reach of the courts?

Commander Stephen Clayman, an officer in the Met's Specialist Crime Command, stated:

> Whilst Al-Fayed is no longer alive to face prosecution, we are determined to bring anyone who is suspected to have played a part in his offending to justice as a result of the inquiry. So far, we have now launched an investigation into a number of people associated with Mohammed Al-Fayed. This investigation will look at what role these individuals may have played in facilitating or enabling his offending, and what opportunities they had to protect victims from his horrendous abuse.
>
> Our priority is to provide justice, answers, and support to those affected by these awful crimes. Given the scale and historic nature of the offending, this investigation is going to take time, but we will approach this case with the integrity, sensitivity, and thoroughness it deserves. To anyone who suffered at the hands of Mohammed Al-Fayed or others who have not yet come forward, I know there may be many reasons why you have not felt able to report the crimes committed against you. I know you may have faced years of silence or disbelief, but you are not alone.

We are here, ready to support you and ensure your voice is heard. Even if you feel your information is small or insignificant, it could make a difference to this investigation. Every voice matters and collectively we can piece together the truth.

Harrods now faces the monumental task of addressing Fayed's crimes. In response to the allegations, current Harrods management has established a support fund for Fayed's victims and pledged full cooperation with police investigations.

A spokesman said: 'The ownership of Harrods changed in 2010 when Fayed sold the business to a Qatari sovereign wealth fund.' The present owners have gone on the record to express their sympathy with anyone who was a victim of Fayed and apologise, emphasising that Harrods today is 'a very different organisation to the one owned and controlled by Fayed' and is now 'one that seeks to put the welfare of their employees at the heart of everything they do'.

'Harrods has put in place a scheme to assist any former or current employees who were abused by Fayed, which includes counselling and fair financial compensation mirroring a court's approach to levels of awards without legal proceedings.'

Dame Jasvinder Sanghera, an expert in supporting sexual offences victims, was appointed as an Independent Survivor Advocate by Harrods. In 2024 Harrods stated that an internal review (supported by external lawyers) was looking at whether any current staff were involved in any of the allegations against Fayed either directly or indirectly and is also in direct communication with the Metropolitan Police to assist with any relevant inquiries. At the time of going to print, the outcomes of Harrods's own internal review and any police investigation were unknown and no current employees have been arrested or charged with any offence.

The newly formed Harrods Survivors support group has become a powerful voice for victims, providing not just mutual support but advocacy for systemic change. Their demands go beyond compensation and counselling, calling for a complete overhaul of corporate governance and accountability structures at Harrods and similar institutions.

The legal battles are just beginning. With Leigh Day solicitors representing multiple survivors in what may become one of the largest civil actions of its kind, Harrods faces years of litigation and public scrutiny.

To those who tried to make a difference; you are the heroes of this story. But the stars are the women, of course. Those who were brave and confident enough to speak out, those with the decency to tell their stories for the sake of other women, indeed for all people of the future.

In their names, changes need to happen.

#MeToo has been a glorious movement, encouraging people to divulge the truth and advocate for one another. It's the only way to ensure proper, long-term change. Speaking out pours light onto problems and stops them from festering in the dark, it pulls pain out of the shadows and exposes it. Speaking out is the way in which we can make the future a better place for everyone.

But we need more than just the truth to be known. We need action.

First, the legal system must evolve to better protect victims and hold perpetrators accountable in the following ways:

1. **Reform of non-disclosure agreements (NDAs):**
   These cursed documents that seek to silence the innocent must be fundamentally reformed. When a document is used to cover up a crime, it's clearly wrong. The UK must follow jurisdictions that have already banned NDAs in cases of sexual harassment and abuse. No legal instrument should ever again be used to shield criminal behaviour.

2. **Extended statutes of limitations:** The unique trauma of sexual violence, coupled with the power imbalances that often prevent immediate reporting, demand extended timelines for seeking justice. The current limits fail to account for the reality that many victims need years to process their trauma before they can come forward.

3. **Protection for whistleblowers:** Strong whistleblower protections must include not just job security but financial security, recognising that speaking truth to power often carries devastating economic consequences. Whistleblowers need both legal and financial shields against retaliation.

4. **Mandatory disclosure of settlement patterns:** Companies should be required to disclose patterns of settlements related to misconduct, even when individual settlements remain confidential. This transparency would help identify systemic problems before they become endemic.

5. **Anti-SLAPP legislation:** The UK desperately needs robust anti-SLAPP legislation to prevent the wealthy and powerful from using legal intimidation to silence victims and journalists. No one should fear financial ruin for speaking truth about abuse.

Second, institutional culture must transform:

1. **Independent reporting mechanisms:** Organisations need truly independent channels for reporting misconduct, separate from management chains that can be compromised by power dynamics.

2. **Corporate accountability:** Boards of directors must be held personally accountable for fostering cultures that enable abuse. Executive compensation should be tied to creating safe workplace environments.

3. **Training and education:** Comprehensive education about consent, appropriate workplace behaviour, and bystander intervention must become standard in all workplaces.

4. **Support for victims:** Organisations must establish trauma-informed protocols for supporting victims who come forward, including access to counselling, legal advice, and career support.

Finally, we must recognise that wealth and power don't exempt anyone from consequence, and open secrets need to be reported and dealt with. Those who worked at the top of Harrods and in the police now face a difficult time, as the juggernaut of the law slowly crunches towards them. We must hope that when it reaches them it exposes everything they did, everything they knew and didn't say, and every secret they hid in order to keep their jobs.

Despite the darkness of this story, there are genuine reasons for hope. The very fact that Fayed's crimes have finally been exposed – that his victims are being heard and believed – illustrates a seismic shift from the culture that protected him for decades.

The survivors who've come forward have already achieved what once seemed impossible: they've shattered the myth of Fayed's untouchability and forced powerful institutions to acknowledge their complicity. Each woman who speaks out makes it easier for others to do the same, creating a cascade effect that is gradually transforming our cultural landscape.

Legal reforms are advancing, albeit slowly. The UK government has begun consulting on limiting the use of NDAs in cases of sexual harassment, and momentum is building for stronger anti-SLAPP protections. These changes, once unimaginable, now seem inevitable as public awareness grows.

Most importantly, the conversation has changed. What was once dismissed as 'the way things are' is now recognised as the crime it always was. New generations are entering workplaces with different expectations about power, respect and accountability.

Belinda's wounds may never fully heal, nor those of countless others who suffered at Fayed's hands. But their courage in speaking out ensures that their pain serves a purpose: the creation of a world where predators like Fayed can no longer operate with impunity.

Only then can we look women like Belinda in the eye and tell her that we're all working hard to make sure this never happens again.

ACKNOWLEDGEMENTS

Huge thanks to everyone at HarperCollins for their help – especially my publisher Katya Shipster for her support and enthusiasm, and Daisy Ward for assistance and encouragement. Tom Jarvis and David Hirst for their legal help, and Mark Bolland for making sure all the right words were in the right order. I am also indebted to Simon Gerratt, chief organiser and coordinator, for all his hard work, and to Chris Kwok and Tom Hill, my crack PR and marketing team. Thanks to everyone who helped – there are so many of you – from cover designers to production controllers and everyone in between.

Thanks also to Gareth Kervin for his incredible help and patience. This project would never have got off the ground without him.

Thanks to Charlie Bronks, Sue Bence, Katherine Wolf, Jools Thompson, Rachel Corner, Daisy Chatterton, Amanda Ohayon and Debra Norton.

There are so many people to acknowledge for their help

with this book. First, to all the women who bravely told their stories; many of whom spoke out for the first time about the horrors they'd endured, motivated by making sure the story was told in full so that no woman has to go through what they endured.

Thanks also to Biggie and the security officers I spoke to – those on the record and those who gave help and advice quietly, showing me notes and playing a recording. Also to the driver who didn't wish to feature in these pages, but whose insight was invaluable.

Thanks to the ex-police officers who helped me to understand the mechanics behind the exploitation that took place, and to those who spoke fully about the systems behind the scenes. Thanks to 'John' and to Hannah Wright, and thanks to Interpol.

Thanks to those with information about Harrods who didn't want to be mentioned in the book – your guidance was helpful. I met a couple at night, at hidden locations, so fearful were they of the consequences of talking, but so determined that the truth should be known.

Thanks to former staff at West Heath School for helping, and for sharing fears you've felt for decades. Thanks to those at the Alexandria National Museum and cultural society, and to Doha Gamal from the University of Cairo.

Thanks to the lawyers at four different law firms representing the women for talking so openly about the cases in their care.

To Dr Patricia Hamilton, Professor Essi Viding, Christine Pratt at the anti-bullying hotline The Samaritans,

NSPCC, Women's Aid, and those in the Women's Studies Unit at Cairo University who went out of their way to help.

A special mention to Rape Crisis, The Havens and The Priory for spending so much time helping me to fully understand the astonishing long-term impact of rape, sexual abuse and bullying.

Thanks to Mitie Security, G4S and PACER (Public Access to Court Electronic Records).

Mark Rowe, editor of *Professional Security Magazine*, Dr Jerry Hart and three government ministers who helped enormously.

And – thanks to all those who went before me . . . Tom Bower for his exceptional biography, *Vanity Fair*, all at *Private Eye* magazine, all the newspapers who have covered the story so thoroughly and sensitively, especially the *Mail on Sunday*. Thanks and well done to the BBC, Channel 4 and ITV for the documentaries that finally kicked down the wall of silence.

Sources used for the book also include government reports, unpublished documents, emails, letters, NDAs and court transcripts. I was shown unpublished articles by journalists who were thrown off course by SLAPPs, and notes from board meetings at Harrods that corroborated what I was being told.

Many of those who contributed to the book did so anonymously. Thank you for your help.

PICTURE CREDITS